BREAKTHROUGH VALUE

Discover *Your* One-Of-A-Kind Value Proposition

Melynn Sight

ISBN: 978-0-578-74665-4 (paperback)
A Kindle e-book format of this book is also available.

Edited by Jayme Gittings, acornandyou.com

Layout by Mary Neighbour, MediaNeighbours

Cover Design by Teresa Mandala, bella-designs.biz

nSight Marketing, Leawood, KS 66206

www.breakthroughvalue.org

www.nsightmarketing.com

To the thousands of association executives, staff, and volunteer leaders who dedicate countless hours to plan for, invest in, and convey the value of membership.

Contents

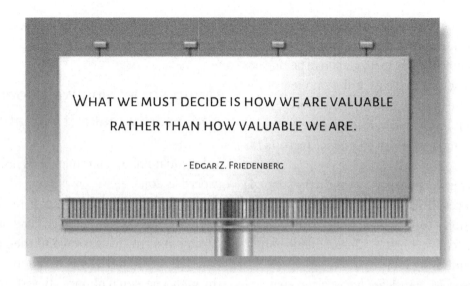

WHAT WE MUST DECIDE IS HOW WE ARE VALUABLE
RATHER THAN HOW VALUABLE WE ARE.

- EDGAR Z. FRIEDENBERG

Introduction

When did you last hear someone say: "Give me one good reason why"?

Years ago, I began asking members across the country for the one main reason they belong to their association. They responded with "my boss said I have to" or "I'm not really sure how to answer that." It left me curious about how universal these responses were. With hundreds of member survey reports at my fingertips, we went on a search to learn more from the very customers I wondered about: the association member.

The data shows that business owners are no more likely to call out one common benefit of membership than a front-line practitioner. The new member appears least confident in their expectations about the one key benefit of membership. While I hesitate to generalize, from our research, few members answer the question the same way for the same association. The findings made me curious: Do leaders have a similar problem identifying one main reason for belonging that would influence members to pay more attention from the day they join throughout their career?

While associations are proud of all that they deliver to members, the hypothesis was that members don't know the one main reason to belong because (1) leaders each have a different view of the association's expertise, and (2) associations focus on tangible relevance (services, tools, events) instead of the most relevant *emotional* reasons for belonging.

In fact, a regular preparatory step in the strategic thinking process involves asking leaders to identify the association's top strategic issue. Common responses are "conveying the value of membership" and "communicating value."

Since association insiders have varying perceptions of the biggest, most significant benefits of membership and the value of belonging to the association, members are consequently on their own to discover what services they get, uncertain what to look for in return for the dues they pay.

Today is a critical time to re-evaluate why your association exists. Modern day business moves fast and brings with it many unknowns that require associations to be nimble and relevant. Market shifts and world events will result in competition for limited resources, which leads to new and evolving choices for members.

This book is your roadmap to crystalize what you do well in light of what your members need most. Along the way, you will explore the key emotional reasons your association matters to your members so you can offer them a relevant rationale for belonging.

Doing something well does not necessarily make it valuable.

Value must link to your member's needs, not your expertise alone.

For a moment, put yourself in the shoes of your customer, a new member. Let's call her Sarah. Sarah joins the profession and then the association. Sarah will initially learn about what you do through a personal phone call, visiting your website, and the new member packet that arrives for Sarah in the mail or the full day orientation session at your office.

In these interactions, Sarah hears and sees all that you do that should help her at some time in her career. Sarah is a captive audience, but the information is overwhelming. Your presentation (or materials) represent a collection of everything Sarah should value.

Roger Turcotte, a respected association colleague, explained to me his analogy about that orientation. After the overview of the association's most important benefits, "the member now thinks that a UPS truck will pull up to the office of the new member's loading dock and deliver fifteen or twenty items that will deliver value and make them successful."

In our example, Sarah is too overwhelmed to look at all that is coming at her. She absorbs everything equally and is unable to prioritize what is important to her at that moment. This first impression misses its power to connect with Sarah with a simple and relevant rationale that relates to her worries and tells her what to expect, with baby steps that offer the next priority benefits over time.

Membership is not a UPS truck. It is a manageable series of installments built over time.

Find and build your association's value.

The product you will produce from this book will become the foundation of your strategy—from the way you think about strategy to the top-level message about the value you deliver. Your new rationale will relate to many different member types and will call out what you do best that they need most. Keep in mind a few reminders:

- You cannot dictate value. When you discover it, you will be on a path to being even more relevant.
- Value is an experience, not a service. You will communicate about your service as a stepping stone to help a member do something more.
- Value is built over time.

- Value happens in every part of your organization.

Once you discover your value from your members' perspective, and the one main reason that you matter to them, your organization will be ready for anything down the road, including your response in a crisis, and tomorrow's definition of "normal."

When your association makes a strategic decision to get to know itself through the eyes of its members, you have the chance to use the promise to develop a new voice (both in words and approach), as well as a philosophy that leads to innovation and intentional change to the status quo.

Throughout this process—from the decision to pursue, to keeping the new promise alive through reinforcement and repetition—a CEO and President will lead a new approach to improve member attention, engagement, and participation.

Laura Crowther, CEO of Coastal Carolinas Association of REALTORS® (CCAR), worked through this process to discover CCAR's value proposition. She offered feedback on why the value proposition led the association to change course:

> This process made us focus and act on what our members find valuable from CCAR, not what we tell them is valuable.

This is a start-to-finish look at how to uncover, define, and then use your value proposition as a strategic asset. The following chapters will blend a focus on your association's strengths with intentional focus on your members.

How the process works from start to finish.

Instead of thinking about the process as a whole, this book breaks the work into three chunks that you can bite off one at a time.

Part 1 will unify you and your team around why it is so hard for an association to unify around one key message. You will learn the definition of a value proposition, how it impacts your brand, and what to do to prepare for the project.

Part 2 is the seven-step process. All the steps are interrelated, like a map to help you discover and then develop the message. This will bring to light how to relay your value differently to influence your diverse membership to pay more attention.

Part 3 answers "now what?" You now have the fresh new message. You will understand how to get your staff and leaders comfortable with the message and will decide together how to best live your new promise to ensure a return on your investment.

The chart on pages 88-89 sets expectations for the timing and roles of the many people who will be part of process. The project plan relates to each of the three parts. You will find a suggested timeline, the group or person who is responsible for each step, and the dependencies between groups to successfully complete the steps that follow.

Part 1:

Boundless Business Benefits

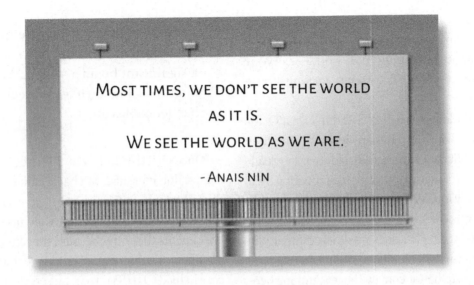

MOST TIMES, WE DON'T SEE THE WORLD
AS IT IS.
WE SEE THE WORLD AS WE ARE.

- ANAIS NIN

The Journey

The longer I work with association communicators, the more I think of the popular quote attributed to Anaïs Nin: "Most times we don't see the world as it is. We see the world as we are."

In over thirty years working with communicators, I hear common questions from staff and executives alike.

- How do we get more clicks?
- How can we get our members to understand everything we have to offer—*all* of our most valuable member benefits?
- How can we reach more members?
- How can we get more readers to pay attention?

All great questions! The better you know and pay attention to your members (both what worries and motivates them) the better you will get at grabbing their dispersed attention and persuading your most distracted, disinterested members to engage in meaningful ways.

When members feel more connected, they are more likely to respond, act, and behave like the association anticipates. However, the only way to connect better is to take a step back and get to know them so well that you know exactly how to get their attention.

To paraphrase, seeing the world—as your members see it—is the first step to making strong connections.

I'm reminded of Michael Readinger, CEO for Council for Health & Human Service Ministries (CHHSM). Michael successfully led their key leaders and a team of members through discovering their value proposition. When Michael stepped into his new position as CEO, he began to initiate change. One of CHHSM's strategic issues was their difficulty in connecting with their members. Their resulting strategic goal was to better convey the few, unique benefits that come with membership. Michael wanted help to discover CHHSM's unique value proposition: to uncover what CHHSM offers members that they cannot get anywhere else but need the most to be successful in their business.

Michael expressed why it is so hard to connect with members:

> So many of our members are disengaged because they are busy dealing with their own issues on their home fronts. They're so focused inside their organization, it's hard for them to look out the window to see us. It's challenging to persuade them that there's something at our association that will help them be more successful or effective, or to overcome a significant business issue. And then, once you make that connection, the barrier comes down.

Once CHHSM followed this process to develop their value message, Michael realized that having the value proposition in-hand gave them the confidence and precise language they needed to share the benefits they offer because they know both their members and their organizations that well. The process helped CHHSM trust, but verify, their priority messages and articulate those messages in a way that all leaders and staff could convey.

While it is impossible for you, as an association communicator, to know every member as an individual, is there a way to learn what a few important member groups need most? Could you challenge yourself to ask better questions regularly and then actively listen to their feedback, both from the promoters and detractors? Could you systematically apply that knowledge to your planning, your communications, and even your interactions?

More eyeballs on your information (and resulting clicks, shares, likes, and interests) do not come from magically choosing the perfect words or images for your communications. True engagement comes from studying your members passionately and responding purposefully to what you learn. Asking intentional, specific questions to important member groups leads to insightful feedback. Purposefully solicited feedback will identify how your organization solves a member's specific problem—instead of a "one size fits all" approach.

Since your communications are a vital asset for both your association and its members, finding words that strengthen your brand are an important tool to set you apart. Communicating a simple, clear message assures members they can rely on you because your association responds to their specific needs. This asset will become a critical success factor for your association.

If you are experiencing the seemingly unsolvable "our members don't know our value," "our members are not engaged," "our members don't read," or "we are not reaching the right people (or enough people) for our latest service, event, or class," then this process can help you overcome those barriers.

A Google search reveals an overwhelming number of ways to develop a value proposition. Most of them begin with advice like: "Take a good look at what you do well." Instead, undertake this process when you are ready to take a new look at discovering the value you deliver from the people who keep you in business: your members.

Put up your antenna and pack up longstanding approaches.

The approach that follows will help you discover what is valuable directly from your most important customers. You will be most successful when you disentangle what you believe you do today that is absolutely, without-a-doubt, valuable to your members. Set it aside. This moment gives you a reason to make room to discover something new you might do well or realize that a minor member benefit actually is more important to your members than you thought. This moment allows you the chance to take a time-out and reaffirm the pledge that *the member matters first*.

You have the chance to reinvent the way your association thinks, plans, and communicates what it does best.

What if I told you that without investing in breaking though the value mystery, you are spending a fortune in wasted resources and time? By choosing to take the time to follow the steps outlined in this book you will serve your members by getting to know them from a very different perspective, using their words and listening to their biggest worries. You will serve your leaders when you establish a united voice that is consistent across your association. Finally, you will serve your staff better when you focus on the one bigger promise beyond planning an individual class, an event, or a member communication.

Define value from the member's eyes.

To put your expectations in the right place, our approach focuses solely on the member from start to finish.

Let's take a minute or two to talk about the uninvolved member. Not someone on a committee and not a volunteer. Uninvolved means that the member is either too new to know much about what you offer, or they have never had the experience (or occasion) to invest more time in the association.

Getting their attention is part "cutting through the clutter" and part relating to them about something they care about. You can get their attention when you overcome a significant worry or offer a solution, an answer, or an experience to help them do business better.

We begin with member worries because when we inquire about a worry, the root is usually something emotional and not material. For example, workshop members typically answer with responses like, "I worry about my competition," or "I worry about not being up-to-date with all that is going on in my industry," or "I don't know where my future business is coming from."

Value is in the member's mind. Value is what they feel when they experience your service, offering, or people. Value is the result of what you say or do that makes the member feel more confident, competent, or credible.

Like most associations, it is likely that your association's service portfolio was built over time and has grown to dozens of service areas. In our work with new and uninvolved members, it only takes one emotional reason and a few tangible benefits to show a member how you deliver on your claim of value. You can be known for something more than classes, events, lobbying, or technology.

When you present an emotional solution, you have a hook to get your distracted member's attention. For example, knowledge of the laws could help a member be more credible in their business. Credibility is an *emotional*, not a *tangible*, offering. Alternatively, efficiency in technology or tools could help speed up a member's business process. Technology is the tangible offering (the service), but the benefit is work-life balance. A solution expresses what happens as a direct result of those offerings.

There are many approaches to developing a value proposition. Many begin with "assessing your strengths." There are respected authors, consultants, and association executives who believe the starting point is a list of the services and programs that the association does well today.

We take the opposite approach. We set the association's strengths aside and begin with the member.

In the chapters ahead, I will lay out *what is in it for you*, the Association Executive, Communications Director, or Board President. I will remind you *why* and then explain in detail *how* to discover your own unique member value proposition. You will learn:

1. what a value proposition is (and isn't);
2. how to discover and craft one for your association; and,
3. how to plan to deliver, build on, and be known for your unique promise of value.

Yes, your value proposition will highlight your strengths. In fact, it will focus on your differentiators. But it will lead first with what the members need most. Then it will link to what your association does best that members cannot get anywhere else. And because you deliver on your claim so well, it conveys why members are better off *with* than *without* you.

The message will boost your credibility. If you are willing to embrace this work, you are about to experience an inspiring approach to strengthening your brand. You will have a basis for *planned and authentic member communications* based on what *they* need the most. You will think, behave, and speak differently. You will connect with more of your members—beyond those who already believe in you.

How to use this book.

This is not intended to be a bookshelf book. It is intentionally the size, shape, and layout of a workbook. As you make your way through the book, feel free to write in the margins and use the book as your partner for brainstorming how you could approach the project.

Begin by reading this book once, all the way through, in a quiet place to get familiar with the work ahead, the concepts, and the scope of the process.

When you decide to share this idea with your board, you should provide a copy to those who are interested to learn more. You can also visit www.breakthroughvalue.org for an on-demand presentation of the process to help your leadership learn more about a value proposition project.

Once you decide this project is right for your association, a task force will be the group to take on the work. It will help them to have a copy of the book to read and then take action together. Like in a cooking class, I will explain and demonstrate; then it is time to gather and discuss, deliberate, or take action as a group.

Additional resources are available at www.breakthroughvalue.org, including an optional "Beyond the Book" resource that provides additional guidance for many of the steps covered in the book.

The value proposition process consists of seven *interdependent* steps. If you skip one, you will work faster, but you will also sacrifice the finished product.

Consider each step as a milestone that helps you better know your association by better understanding your members' needs and how your association can better solve them.

Timing to complete this project from start to finish.

The entire process may take anywhere from ninety days, if you are focused, to six months. Do not let it go longer. The project will lose steam and your task force will lose interest.

Expect to invest in five or more meetings, each for a specific purpose. Throughout the book, you will see the estimated time for each step, how best to use the task force, and who is involved in each step. Designate one person who understands the steps involved to lead the project and keep it moving.

At the end of the book, there is a recommended project plan that offers suggested timing for each step of the process.

THE STRONGEST BRANDS

ANY PERSON, PLACE, ORGANIZATION, OR PRODUCT
FOR WHICH PEOPLE BELIEVE THERE IS
NO SUBSTITUTE.

Value proposition is a brand-booster

Think about the brands you love in your life. The people, places, organizations, and things for which—for you—there are no substitutes. Why do you feel that way? Why are you loyal to those brands?

To help you think through this idea, I would like to tell a brand story that is not related to the business of associations.

When I think about a service that is heads above the rest, my example is my nail professional, Mel.

Mel does not have a complicated business model and her value proposition is very clear. But there *is* a lot of competition, including other businesses offering the same services closer to where I live. What is the rationale for choosing Mel and continuing to build our relationship over time? Her value proposition is my rationale for going back every three weeks for more than ten years. Mel delivers more than a service to her clientele: she is reliable, an expert in her field, has an eye on cleanliness, and knows that her level of professionalism matters to her clients.

(Feel free to substitute Mel with others: your dog sitter; a specialty market; your favorite food or drink brand; your go-to brand of shoes; where you choose to worship; professionals such as REALTORS®, financial planners, doctors, and personal trainers. Value propositions are everywhere and equally relevant in everyday life, so let your mind wander.)

Think about *why* you are loyal to that place, product, or provider. What keeps you going back? What is your rationale for who you choose? Is it the price? Is it the quality? Is it the experience? Is it the security, entertainment value, hospitality, or the comfort?

If you say, "it's the cheapest," then cost is what is valuable to you—that is tangible return. If you say, "it's easy and comfortable to work with that person," then ease and comfort represent emotional relevance; how you feel when you interact with that particular brand is important to you.

Connecting with a brand—recognizing value in a brand—is a game changer and a decision-making shortcut.

If you are not sure, I will take you through my thought process with Mel and my expectations for how I spend my personal time.

- Is the drive worth it? Yes, even though it takes me thirty minutes to get to and from her salon.

- Is she excellent at what she does? Yes, I think she is an expert at what she does.
- Does she take me on time? Yes, I never have to wait.
- Is her space clean and welcoming? Yes, Mel takes every precaution for cleanliness and considers it important that her space feels good when I walk in.
- How much does she cost versus someone else? What she charges is fair. She has the emotional and tangible benefits that I am looking for in this category.

While all of this enters my mind, it is not the reason I am loyal to Mel. I choose Mel for the emotional reasons:

- What is her "table-side manner?" Do we have rapport? Do I enjoy interacting with her?
- Do I walk out feeling good?
- After a forty-five-minute conversation with her, did I spend my time well?

In the end, what makes Mel valuable?

When I sit with Mel, I get an exceptional service from someone who knows what I am looking for and knows her expertise: tangible benefits. But equally important is the emotional benefit. I can rely on her. I feel good when I walk in and better when I walk out. As a result, I recommend Mel whenever I have the chance, positioning her to offer this value proposition to more customers like me in the future.

The bigger the business, the more challenging it is to influence every individual. How do you feel paying for a service about which you know little information? The bigger the business, the clearer the value proposition needs to be.

The automotive service AAA is another example of a value proposition that is both relevant and different from competitors. The AAA proposition is that it is there when you get into a bind, on the road or in your driveway. For your membership, you get the emotional benefit of never being alone in an emergency when needing a tow, a flat tire repair, or assistance getting keys out of a locked car, plus other tangible returns like discounts on other products and services, like helpful travel planning.

The AAA value proposition has proven over time to work. I know people who gladly write that AAA membership check every year. They do not think twice.

Consider online shopping at Zappos.com. Today, fast shipping and service is the norm, but back in the year 2000, Zappos was an anomaly. Shoe shopping online was new. As a consumer, my rationale is the same today that is was back in Y2K. Buying shoes online from Zappos was and still is simple, convenient, easy to use, and rich in selections. These are their differentiators. I receive my package the next day without additional shipping fees. This is tangible relevance. The emotional relevance is that when I'm in a rush and order from Zappos, the next day the shoes arrive at my front door, relieving my worry.

They live their promise of next day service every time. That is an emotional benefit for me.

Zappos delivers on their value proposition: reliable service. And their systems are set up to deliver on their brand through their technology, from their supply chain to their policies.

The key selling points for both AAA and Zappos are knowing their target customers' needs and building their businesses around solving those needs.

Like strong for-profit businesses, strong association brands pay attention to differentiating themselves and how their unique offerings answer their customers' biggest needs. They invest in learning about the members they want to attract and how they deliver their value to that member.

Take some time out to think about your competition: Is it another association, educational institution, or networking or mastermind groups? Do you compete with other associations that attract some of the same members as you? Or does a bigger industry organization command more attention in your industry?

All associations experience at least some competition for members.

Carol Platt, a former CEO for an association in Florida, explained competition this way:

> Think about it: it's a challenge for a small association to compete with mega associations who provide similar offerings in

the same industry. When you survive in the shadow of a well-funded, well-run giant—you survive by delivering something of real value, and members know it. If you deliver the same—then why would they bother with you? The sooner you can discover, and then deliver and communicate what you do that's different to deliver real value, the easier it will be for David to slay Goliath.

This is a chance to get to know your association and discover the highest priority solutions you offer a member. In doing so, you can better influence new members and those more challenging, indifferent, or distracted ones.

Why is your member better with than without you?

You are the brand ambassador, which puts you in a strategic position in your organization. It also means you are the primary salesperson.

For anyone who did not grow up in sales or around the sales process, there are a few fundamental skills that make for successful selling:

- Know your product better than anyone.
- Know your organization's story and brand—and what makes it unique.

- Know your competition
- Listen to understand the prospect's problem and what solutions you might offer
- Establish a relationship with your prospect that makes you the one they think of when they are ready to buy
- Practice the pitch once you know your prospect's situation
- Use persuasive words that offer a solution to their problem
- Make your explanation simple

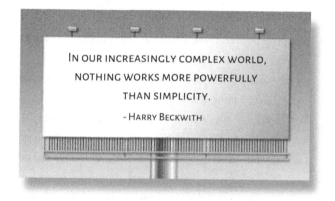

IN OUR INCREASINGLY COMPLEX WORLD, NOTHING WORKS MORE POWERFULLY THAN SIMPLICITY.
- HARRY BECKWITH

But "selling," you might ask? What does sales have to do with the association business?

Stop for a minute and think about this: sales *is the process of establishing credibility and rapport to further a relationship.* In other words, sales is the story-telling engine that moves someone to take action—such as contribute to your political action fund, join, or raise their hand to volunteer.

There is an element of sales in promoting every association event, class, and piece of content included in your communications. Each call to action should sear your value into members' minds.

With that as perspective, I hope you agree that everyone working on behalf of your association is in sales.

Strong brands make selling easier, even for associations.

If you are still not quite sure why your association needs a value proposition today, then consider this: You serve a large percentage of members who are struggling to connect with how you can help them operate better, easier, or with less risk. Like it or not, when a member looks at your logo or sees your name in the inbox, they recall something about you: a memory of an experience, a perception of a third party, or an opinion of your reputation in the industry. Maybe their response is positive; maybe it is not; or possibly they do not know what to think.

Ideally, a strong brand establishes a positive emotional connection. The strongest brand is an emotional shortcut that says the customer is better with than without the product or service. Think of brands you love and consider rereading this paragraph so that you really get the definition of a brand. Your association is a brand.

David Vinjamuri shares in his book, *Accidental Branding*:

> Strong brands solve someone's problem or make their life better or more fun . . . the strongest brands are the result of a narrative that shows your expertise, authenticity, and consistency in a way that relates directly to your target audience.

To influence member perception—to get them to act, contribute, or attend—you will not win them over by simply announcing to all that *your organization* is really good or telling them what *you* want them to do. To get better results, do just the opposite: talk about how your expertise *helps them* achieve a better outcome, improve a skill, or avoid problems in the future.

In other words, be specific and clear about how your solution will help them achieve their goals.

FOCUS ON THE SOLUTION YOU OFFER, NOT THE SERVICE YOU PROVIDE.

Create an impact in your business.

What would you do:

- If 80 percent of your membership were involved, relied on you for the answers, volunteered, contributed above their standard dues to keep your industry healthy, and gave association referrals to non-members every day?

- If 100 percent of your membership were equally committed to intentionally and actively building their personal knowledge to be the best in their industry and relied solely on you to give them an edge in their business?

How would that change your focus?

How would your thinking and planning change if you could entice a large group of non-members that they are better with than without you?

When your sales force is unified around a simple, common message of value that resonates with your members and answers *why your association should matter*, results like these are possible.

Think of a value proposition as a tool that helps you convey an authentic promise. Turn your promise into words to help you sell your strengths with clear, simple language that relates directly to your target audience and beyond.

Getting their attention with your value proposition.

According to Jeffrey Slater, author of the *Marketing Sage*, "what your strategic marketing plan describes in detail, your value proposition says in a few words."

Associations can mistake a list of association features—such as their services, tools, resources, events, and discounts—as a value proposition. Each of these are individual features that you hope will get your membership's attention. But they all contribute to a bigger reason for a member to belong.

Think about something your association has invested in, like a new software tool, a class, or an event. The feature describes the product or service. The benefit states the result of the feature: how the member could, for example, save time, lower their risk, or be more relevant in order to conduct better business.

Why are benefits so important? They help to overcome many barriers.

- Distraction: members who are busy focusing on managing their business, so they are not paying attention.
- Indifference: members who have few or no expectations of you.
- Overload: members who are turned off because

so much information is not relevant, too complicated, or not useful.

Offering members a laundry list of services does not create more value; instead it leads to overload.

In their *2018 Association Communications Benchmarking Report*, Naylor and Associates observed, "Associations greatly underestimate the impact of communications overload and clutter on the value of membership." Focusing your communications on the features, without connecting the dots about why they matter, leaves members abandoning e-news, scrolling past the social post, and ignoring the very same offerings you, the association communicator, think are most valuable.

A value proposition is one clear, simple statement that helps you:

- Get the member's attention through something you know they need,
- Set your association apart from competitors, and
- Set an expectation for what a member should receive from you.

Value is in the members' minds.

Instead of convincing them what you think *they should value*, remember that value is theirs to decide. They are not thinking to themselves, "I need to take classes, call a legal hotline, or attend events" to be more successful. Their internal voice says, help me "lower my risk," "get more efficient or credible," "make my first (or next) sale," "help me out of a bind," or "market myself better." An association that is clear about how they solve these problems will get attention!

When communications go beyond reporting the news or making the announcement about association programs and focus on the benefit, communications staff will evolve from content-creators to attention-creators.

The connection happens when your offering links up as a solution to one of their worries and piques their interest. Once you draw them in with one emotional benefit and something they get from your association that they cannot get anywhere else, you will have a member who is open to and curious about what else you have to offer them.

In a recent workshop, a long-time member, Carolyn, retold a quote she always thought of that explains why their association misses the chance to connect with the uninvolved, busy member. She said, "You can lead a horse to water, but you can't make it drink, unless you make it thirsty."

A clear, simple value proposition is a tool that makes a member pay attention, so that they have a thirst to learn more.

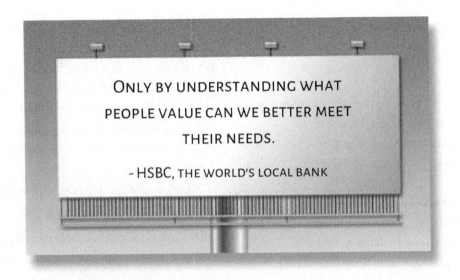

ONLY BY UNDERSTANDING WHAT PEOPLE VALUE CAN WE BETTER MEET THEIR NEEDS.

- HSBC, THE WORLD'S LOCAL BANK

What makes a strong value proposition?

I was walking through Times Square in New York City one afternoon as the sun was setting. Suddenly, blocks and blocks of famous billboards illuminated simultaneously. I looked up and caught a glimpse of an HSBC billboard that said in one sentence how to uncover a strong value proposition: "Only by understanding what people value can we better meet their needs."

How do you figure out what people value?

The simplest way to uncover value is to (1) decide who you want to influence, (2) find the uninformed who you want to enlighten, and (3) persuade those people to talk to you. If you can complete those three steps, you have the chance to ask the right questions to help you discover the link between their worries and how your association can address them.

A value proposition is the rationale to invest.

A rationale is what goes through the member's mind as they consider your association's offer.

The statement packs a lot into one short message. It is the closest thing to a sales pitch you will ever create for your association.

The value proposition becomes a powerful combination of "facts plus feelings" that focuses on how your member will have their needs met, articulated in one short, simple statement. Keep these tips in mind:

- *Set aside* how long you have been in business, your premier services, or your robust list of member benefits that lives on your membership landing page. These will not effectively get a distracted (or new) member's attention.
- *Lead with what they care about.* This requires that you disentangle from what you believe are your association's biggest strengths right now.
- *Stay centered on the member* and what they can achieve with your services that they cannot get anywhere else.
- *Focus on your members' emotional needs* and not necessarily a list of all the services you offer.

WordStream, an online advertising firm, recently presented two examples of strong value propositions.

They each offer customers an emotional rationale. I marked the following examples to show the emotional rationale (ER), followed by the proof points (PP), tangible ways the company delivers on the claim. While each company likely delivers many other ancillary benefits of their product, they narrow their focus to what is most relevant to the prospect.

Slack – *Be More Productive at Work with Less Effort* (ER)

- All your project tools in one place (PP)
- Simple to use application across every mobile platform (PP)
- Encourages direct collaboration with your team (PP)

Uber – *The Smartest Way to Get Around.* (ER)
- One tap and a car comes directly to you (PP)
- Our driver knows exactly where to go (PP)
- Payment is completely cashless (PP)

Without explicitly saying so, Uber highlights everything that differentiates them from a traditional taxi and points out how its service is better.

A third example is a personal one. It is a boutique hotel and guesthouse in my hometown of Kansas City.

No Vacancy – *The backdrop for life's most meaningful moments.* (ER)

- We give you space but we are here when you need us. (PP)
- Furnished like a well-appointed loft with consistency of a boutique hotel. (PP)
- Make it your own personal guest house. (PP)

Each of these propositions presents the simple, clear language of the necessary components of a strong value proposition.

1. Resonate: Explain how the offering is relevant to the customer.
2. Differentiate: Show how the offering is unique.
3. Substantiate: State in clear, simple language how the offering is delivered today.

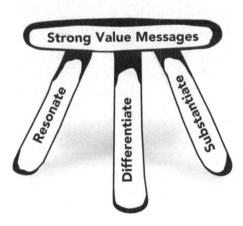

When an association's claim focuses on features.

Creating a strong value proposition is not easy and can miss the mark even with the best intentions. I asked one association, "What one benefit does your association deliver very well today that your members need most—and that they cannot get anywhere else?" They answered:

Association's Response

Membership with us has a direct impact on a member's financial bottom line through our legal, tech, and other resources.

Their answer was part mission statement, part a summary of services. There are three key reasons this response was a missed chance to relay a relevant message of value.

1. *Internal in focus*. Notice the statement begins with a reference to "Membership with us" (the association). It describes what the association believes they do well, but does not say what they solve or achieve for the member.
2. *Lacks differentiation*. This description could be any statement from any association. If you could insert anyone else's name into the

statement, it is not strong enough to get your members' attention. A strong value message is specific to the association's unique expertise.

3. *Lacks substance*. The statement offers *claims*; yet does not solve a particular problem; a member should read the message and immediately understand "what is in it for me, the new member?" or "what is in it for me, the business owner?"

This message *declares* what the association does, yet it *reveals* nothing about how the member will benefit. Remember: the sole purpose of a value message is to *link what members need most with what you do best*.

Terri Langhans, in her book, *The 7 Marketing Mistakes Every Business Makes*, cautions organizations: "Don't breathe too much of your own exhaust."

You cannot create a value proposition in the boardroom. The strongest value proposition comes from discovery, input, and perspective from the people who hold a stake in your association's future. Your members are your stakeholders.

Case Study: The ValYOU Proposition.

Michael Readinger, the CEO mentioned earlier from CHHSM, coined the process their "ValYOU proposition." In his words:

It's all about them: the member. It's a discovery about what keeps them up at night, and then presents our fact-inspired solution through our association's strategy, our member strategy, our new member process, our communications strategy, our engagement strategy, all the way through our programs and services.

Below is what CHHSM members saw in their new member materials when they joined the association *before* they embarked on discovering their value proposition. The list is exhaustive, and likely overwhelming to the new or prospective member.

BENEFITS OF
MEMBERSHIP

COUNCIL for HEALTH and HUMAN SERVICES MINISTRIES
United Church of Christ

Tangible benefits of joining and being a member in good standing of CHHSM:

- Listing in United Church of Christ (UCC) Yearbook and inclusion under the Church's Federal non-profit tax exemption, qualifying your ministry for "Church Plan" status.
- Listing in CHHSM's cross-referenced, on-line directory of UCC-related service providers at www.chhsm.org, which includes links to the websites of CHHSM member ministries.
- Eligibility to have two voting delegates at the CHHSM annual membership meeting.
- Access to CHHSM store, our group purchasing plan that offers significant savings on a wide variety of products and special discount programs for member ministry employees.
- Receipt of, and access to, news and promotion through CHHSM's electronic resources, including our monthly e-newsletter - Diakonie.
- Eligibility for any employee of member ministries to participate in CHHSM's customized leadership formation programs and events.
- Access to free planned giving through CHHSM's Planned Giving Partnership with UCC Financial Development Ministries.
- Eligibility to participate in the Nollau Institute, CHHSM's leadership formation program that offers specialized education and theological reflection for faith-based servant leaders. Nollau Institute graduates qualify for consecration as CHHAM Diakonal Ministers, and become part of the dynamic CHHSM Minister Community.
- Eligibility to participate in CHHSM Health – affordable, comprehensive health care, dental care, mental health and substance abuse services and pharmaceutical services (offered in covenant with the Pension Boards UCC).
- Access to CHHSM Rx, a stand-alone prescription drug plan for employees of CHHSM member ministries
- Eligibility to post job announcements in CHHSM's on-line Vocations Opportunities Listing to reach a national Audience.
- Access to CHHSM's public policy advocacy resources, offered in collaboration with a network of health and human service advocacy partners in Washington, D.C.
- Eligibility to participate in pension accumulation plans with the Pension Boards UCC. Access to CHHSM's expertise and customized programs on the management and governance of faith-based service organizations.

Other valuable benefits of CHHSM membership are less tangible:

- Being part of an intimate community of colleagues who share values and a vocational calling to advance the healing and service ministry of Jesus Christ.
- Participating in meaningful dialogues about enhancing self-care, solving problems, best practices, conflict resolution and programmatic development.
- Consulting with CHHSM's professional staff whose competencies include organizational analysis, management, theology, marketing, communications, social media and business development.
- Informing, and being informed by the United Church of Christ's public policy positions on critical social, ethical and regulatory issues in health and human services.
- Devising strategies with colleagues to enhance church relationships and expand awareness of our common mission at all levels of the United Church of Christ.
- Using the creative resources and networking capacities of CHHSM to expand awareness of, and support for your ministry.

CHHSM discovered and then developed a new message by learning what members need most and why a new member should pay attention. This is the teaser message that they show to new members today, so members know what to expect, and they build from this simple message to draw the member in to learn more:

A member's updated first impression of CHHSM provides clear, simple language about why leaders of their ministries should pay attention—because CHHSM is a collection of inspiring leaders with a bold vision who have shared values. Members relate to other members who share common challenges and a similar vision for their respective member ministries.

The short message, with three examples that we call proof points, supports the emotional benefits of belonging. This is emotional relevance. The three "action words" represent specific programs and benefits that CHHSM delivers today that answer their members' biggest needs.

Once they agreed on the message, it became a cornerstone for the way CHHSM lives up to their promise: in every conversation, in the boardroom, during strategic planning, in staff meetings, and through member communications.

Deliver a money moment.

I once gave a keynote talk to a group of association leaders to present the value proposition concept. Andrea Bowles was an association leader in the audience who related to the concept herself in her own business. After the session, Andrea came up to me and said, "Today I had a money moment." Curious, I asked her to explain.

Andrea said at one point in the middle of the explanation something clicked. She said to herself, "I can see how this organization *can help me make more money*—after hearing about their value proposition. Learning about it was worth my two-hour investment in this meeting. It was my money moment."

A VALUE PROPOSITION:
YOUR UMBRELLA MESSAGE
- THE ONE BIG REASON
THEY SHOULD BELONG.

ONE KEY EMOTIONAL BENEFIT PLUS
A FEW TANGIBLE EXAMPLES THAT
PROVE YOU ARE THE BEST
AT ANSWERING THEIR BIGGEST NEEDS.

Agree on what this project will solve

One of my favorite songs from the 70's, "Tin Man" by America, contained a hook that always hit home with me as a metaphor for a value proposition. "Oz never did give nothing to the Tin Man that he didn't, didn't already have."

A value proposition will (likely) not change your association's direction or your mission. Instead, you will more likely convey what you do today in a completely different way, shifting to a focus on the member's language instead of your own.

So why do you need one?

The executives who seek our help for this work do it because of a range of common dilemmas:

- The association delivers a range of services, tools, and other offerings, but members still say, "I don't know what I get for my membership."

- It is time to reevaluate exactly what the association should focus on, including the right levels of financial resources, manpower, and focus.

- The association wants to identify, and then agree on, the most relevant and compelling reasons they exist so that staff and leaders can present a unified and consistent message to their stakeholders.
- The association is under a competitive threat or aims to grow, creating a pressing need to reinvent themselves for tomorrow's member.
- A strategic priority such as "grow engagement with," "get more attention from," or "be more relevant to" current and prospective members.
- Members are disconnected from what the association does to positively impact their business.

Imagine what happens when your entire staff and leadership team owns a common message? How powerful would it be to overhear each staff member and leader express your value message in their own words? What next milestone would be unlocked if every person on your team was comfortable articulating why your association matters and how they fit into the solution?

Settle on your guiding why.

There are different questions associations ask themselves when considering taking on developing a value proposition:

- Could it help you move forward a strategic goal?
- Would it help you attract more members?
- Would it help you persuade more members to get involved or support member retention?

When your leaders are unified about what problem this project will solve, you will get more traction throughout the process.

You will want support from your full board, even though they will not be an active part of the process. You will also need their *confidence* in the process, *endorsement* of the outcome, and *empowerment* to let them own the work.

Okay, enough background. Let's get to work.

Welcome to a blueprint to discover your association's strengths from your member's viewpoint and your one-of-a-kind value for yourself.

Action (For Your Board or Executive Committee):

Let's assume you and I are at one of our association events at the expo hall, where all of our members are looking for information and shopping for some of our most valuable tools. Assume that we are manning the booth.

A new member walks up to the display and asks, "What does your association offer me that I can't get anywhere else to help me make significant progress in my career?"

What is the first thing you would say?

Ask each person to write their answer on an index card without any name. Collect them and hold them for later. Once the process is complete, then relook at the cards to compare to the new message that your members help to create. We'll talk about this again at the end of the process, in Part 3.

Your Action Notes:

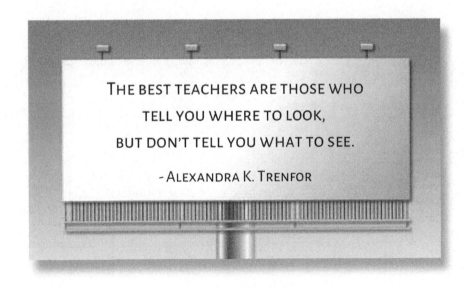

THE BEST TEACHERS ARE THOSE WHO
TELL YOU WHERE TO LOOK,
BUT DON'T TELL YOU WHAT TO SEE.

- ALEXANDRA K. TRENFOR

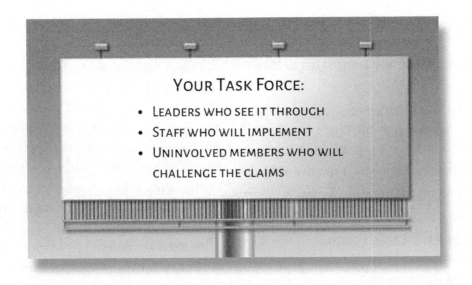

YOUR TASK FORCE:

- LEADERS WHO SEE IT THROUGH
- STAFF WHO WILL IMPLEMENT
- UNINVOLVED MEMBERS WHO WILL CHALLENGE THE CLAIMS

Assemble your task force

Preparing for the project is a critical first step. The team that works on this project will influence its success.

As you think about assembling your task force, remember that previously uninvolved members will help you discover the most relevant new perspectives. While it might be uncomfortable to think that unfamiliar faces will be a dependency for success and the bulk of your members on the task force, you will appreciate it in the end. These members will help you see the association from an outsider's point of view.

Consider at least fifteen people, including:

- Chief staff executive (e.g., CEO, Executive Director),
- President and/or President-Elect (Chair and/or Chair-Elect) of the board of directors,
- one or two key staff members (especially your communications director, if you have one),

- at least ten full-time, uninvolved members (from many diverse member groups), and
- a member or affiliate member who is a creative thinker.

A reminder: This is not a process for your "kool-aid drinkers," nor for your full board of directors or entire staff. A diverse group of those who have a range of knowledge about your expertise will balance out the process.

The role of the task force.

Your task force should be clear about their role in this project. Here is a short list:

- *To deconstruct* what the association thinks are their strongest member benefits—set them aside for just a little while and focus on the member.
- *To listen to (and to speak openly about)* what uninvolved members worry about most in their work—get a full look at the solutions you are aiming to present since you will want them to talk freely about what keeps them up at night.
- *To be honest* in linking your association's expertise to their needs.
- *To think like they think*—or the new, prospective, or uneducated member.

- *To reconstruct value* from the members' perspective.

Except for your members, leaders will need to "get on the balcony" throughout this project. In the article, *Leading Adaptive Change*, Ron Heifetz describes this perspective as "the ability to view the situation and the responses of participants from a mental 'balcony,' from which one can see patterns, minimize one's own emotional responses, and react in ways that will help the community engage in the adaptive challenge."

Heifetz continues that "adaptive change (1) requires new learning than what leaders traditionally believe, and (2) places the responsibility for the solution with the followers."

The process will work best when leaders step away from the details, observe the big picture, and give uninvolved members of the task force the chance to speak up about what they need from their perspective. Encourage leaders to protect and respect the people who speak their truth. It is these voices that will help you discover your value.

Uninvolved members on the task force will help you validate that you are focusing on the member. They will challenge you when you claim that a service or product is important to members—or you believe you deliver a service with expertise, and they perceive otherwise. Uninvolved members will challenge you if you slip into reinforcing what the association thinks is important.

Kit Fitzgerald, President of the first association to complete a value proposition project using this process, was determined to be open-minded and "question everything" during her presidential year, with no preconception about the outcome. Once the process was complete, Kit looked back with pride: "I feel energized and refreshed from looking at the association from a completely different perspective. This was the best way possible to question everything."

Action: Assemble your task force.

- Determine who will make up your task force. Fifteen people is a minimum-size group. Use the list earlier in this chapter so you recruit the right profile to add value to the project.
- Determine who will chair your task force. It is their job to stay true to the steps in the process and keep the project moving forward. Sometimes this is a committee chair and other times it is the CEO.

Your Action Notes:

Part 2:

Seven Sequential and Significant Steps

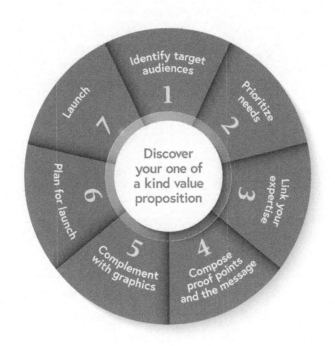

POWERFUL MARKETING PROGRAMS
BEGIN WITH CAREFULLY SELECTING
YOUR TARGET AUDIENCE.

Step 1. Brainstorm, then target your audience

Nothing is more important as you begin this process than identifying the member groups that are most important to the future of your association.

Everyone is not your target audience for this project, even though your message will be intended for all members.

Early in my marketing career, I learned why prioritizing target audiences is so important.

Sometimes it is true: a picture says what words cannot.

In a workshop many years ago, I heard this question, "Would you ask a bunny rabbit for money the same way you would ask a business owner?" I realized, "Of course, I wouldn't!" Each member group has different worries and motivations and needs.

Marketing guru Michael A. Goodman reinforces this advice:

> Start by defining your target audience very precisely—the narrower and more specific the better. Learn what makes them tick, how they think, what they value, their attitudes, habits, practices, needs, current experiences, emotional connections, even the words they use when they discuss your category and their unmet needs.

Put a specific member type inside your head.

Consider all the various groups that make up your membership: tenure as a member, position in the member firm, career background, age, or generation category. These are just a few. Each membership type reacts to, and is motivated by, different solutions. Each group has different experiences depending on their role, so we are going to work to find common needs among them. Finding commonalities between a few recognizably different member groups will help you be more relevant to more members beyond the few member groups that you choose. My colleague Carol Platt calls this the "influential bleed"; in other words, the message spreads much further than those initial three groups.

Try to relate to everyone and you will relate to no one.

My favorite example of targeting a specific audience is from a short little book called *The 7 Marketing Mistakes Every Business Makes*, by Terri Langhans.

One of Terri's marketing fixes says this: "Before you can convince someone you're the right choice, you have to connect to something they care about. Which we know isn't about you. It's about them."

When talking about a target audience, be specific. Terri tells the following story to illustrate how specific you should be during this process:

In their commercial, AT&T showed a working mom packing lunches, getting ready for work with her two little girls skipping around her in the kitchen. One of the little girls asks sweetly: "Mom, don't go to work today. Take us to the beach. Puhleeeeeeze!" Mom says "Sorry sweetie, I can't take you to the beach. I have an important client meeting."

After a sad moment of reflection, and then reluctant acceptance, the little girl asks, "mommy, when I grow up, can I be an important client?"

Gulp. Choke. . . .

In the next scene, mom and her girls are on the beach. Mom is talking on her cell phone. The girls are skipping around her beach chair singing "We're having a meeting, we're having a meeting."

AT&T connected to a specific target audience—working moms and uncovered something valuable that a mom cares most about.

Many people assume that choosing a target audience will limit a marketing message; in fact, it does just the opposite. Being specific about one or more target groups will offer the prospective customer a solution they can relate to, even if they aren't a member of the target audience of buyers. In your case, clarity about the solution you provide one member group will help others rationalize how you can help them, too.

Another example is Apple, whose campaign target market was a young, carefree, and connected group.

Forty years later, Apple can show that their actual customer base still successfully hits that mark and extends well beyond this group of people. While we all may not consider ourselves part of this category, don't we all want to be young, hip, carefree, and connected? This is an example that targeting your audience will help you extend your reach and relate to many other groups beyond your targets. This is what we mean by influential bleed: the chance for you to reach members beyond your initial target groups.

Once you compile a full list of every possible member group, you will narrow it down to three. Yes, the more different those three groups are, the better!

We will refer to a real-life value proposition project throughout the book as an example. This association supports the energy industry, ASEA (a fictional name to protect their confidentiality). This is their actual experience and their process is real.

ASEA's initial response to "Who are your most important member groups?" included:

1. individual professionals and consumers, and
2. companies.

In my workshops, one of the most common responses to the question about an association's most important member groups are the two highest-level groups: either members and non-members or, in this case, individuals and companies. But this is not specific enough. It is impossible to know the breadth of large, generic groups of members. Like choosing *male* and *female* as target groups, the population is simply too broad to draw out a few common needs.

They went back and brainstormed a list of thirteen types of individual professionals/consumers and eight types of companies. With a list of twenty-one groups of members, they followed the process mentioned next, to home in on three target member groups who were especially important to the association:

1. Adopters (pro-energy adopters who endorse the cause for the sake of the environment)
2. Attorneys (an important audience for their regulatory work)
3. Energy company CEOs

It's now time for you to select your target member groups.

Step 1 Action: Prioritize three member groups who are most important to your association's success.

- Brainstorm a list of a dozen or more distinct member groups including, and beyond, traditional member groups. Consider "tech-savvy members," "members on the cusp of business success," or "high producers."
- Be specific: assign a position type, years in business, business size, or income range.
- Use the filtering guidelines you see in the next graphic to prioritize the groups.
- Come to consensus on three member groups. The more unique they are the better.

NOTE:

- This step is for the entire task force.
- Timing: one hour
- It is not necessary to include non-members. A non-member is a company or individual who may have the same worries and needs as a member but has not joined yet.

Steps to Segmentation.

EVERYONE is not a target audience. Try using these filters to narrow down your target to 3 groups.

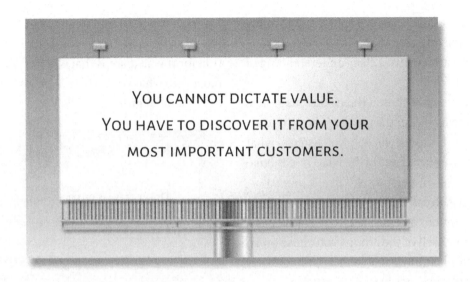

YOU CANNOT DICTATE VALUE.
YOU HAVE TO DISCOVER IT FROM YOUR
MOST IMPORTANT CUSTOMERS.

Step 2.
Listen to their worries and prioritize their needs

The website, *Art of Charm*, suggests four ways to best make connections with others:

1. Practice active listening.
2. Connect on an emotional level.
3. Focus on the other person with questions.
4. Pay attention to how others are speaking.

The value proposition discovery begins with these four insights that set the rules before getting started. The process is completely about the uninvolved members, not the organization, the President, or anyone else in the room.

Strong brands put their strongest customer benefits to the side and invest in getting to know their target audience. Harry Beckwith says in his book *Selling the Invisible*, "Sales is where your marketing must start . . . with a clear understanding of a worried soul."

Now that you have chosen three different groups of members to focus on; the next step is to conduct some research. This step will help you listen to what is going on in their heads and in their day-to-day business lives, from their perspective. To discover value, the next step is to ask a few open-ended questions with no expectations and just listen to what they say.

Get to know each of the groups you chose on an intellectual and emotional level; learn about their work, worries, and needs in their own voice.

Uninvolved members make all the difference in the success of this project.

- To discover member value, you will get your most unbiased perspective from members who do not know or understand your portfolio of benefits. So it is the staff and leaders' job to listen and avoid offering comments or opinions during the next step.
- Uninvolved members may find your interest in them refreshing. They may thank *you* for the chance to participate and share what is most on their minds about their profession.

You cannot tell members what to worry about; but, with an open mind, you will uncover information for the next steps that will link what they need most with what you do best. Worries will vary across each member group.

DON'T TELL ME WHAT I SHOULD VALUE.

SINCERELY, YOUR MEMBER

The worries should be persistent, not circumstantial.

Top-of-mind worries change over time and can impact the dialogue in this step. Prior to 2020, we rarely heard an uninvolved member-at-large offer the worry "advocacy." Or the results of legislation and regulations on their business. Many associations focus a significant amount of resources and manpower on their advocacy strategy. Advocacy is an invisible member benefit unless the association is in the regulation business (like our sample association who is in the energy business, which is highly regulated). Regulations become a significant worry during a world health or economic crisis, when governmental regulation impacts their every-day business life. Involvement in politics takes on a new meaning in a crisis where the members' business activities, and their livelihood are at risk.

Divide your task force into 3 teams (include everyone).

Create a team to represent each target member group from step one. Make sure there is at least one person on each team who fits the profile of that team's target audience. While each member may not be an *actual* member of that target audience, ask the group to step into the shoes of that member-type throughout this part of the process.

The three groups will go to separate areas for the next activity. You can set the time (usually thirty minutes) to brainstorm worries and then narrow that full list down to the most important three to five.

Step 2 Action (part 1):

With all task force members participating, pose this question for each group to answer:

"In your business today, what is the one biggest worry that keeps you up at night?"

Send them off in their groups and reconvene to collect the responses.

NOTE:

- This step is for the entire task force.
- Timing: 30 minutes

When you come back together to debrief with the entire group about each group's worries, someone will record all of the worries for all members to see. Don't put words into their heads (unless you need to clarify), but use the question "why?" freely!

Once you review and document all the worries from each of the three groups, send participants back for part two: selecting the five biggest needs to help members overcome their worries.

Step 2 Action (part 2):

Think about that biggest worries you listed before. If anything were possible . . . what do you need to overcome that worry?

Ask them to prioritize their needs. Come back together to review responses.

NOTE:

- This step is for the entire task force.
- Timing: thirty minutes to one hour

These responses came from the question, "What is the one business worry that keeps you up at night?"

Target Audience Worries		
Adopters	Attorneys	Company CEOs
Will I have power when I need it?	Loss of billable hours from loss of customers	Legislative and regularity concerns
Have we done enough for the future generations?	Where does my future work come from?	Competition in the market
Will there be cost control or will the charges spike anytime?	Will time spent pursuing this business offer enough return?	Access to capital when tax credits sunset
Am I part of the majority who want this? (social anxiety)	Not being current on policy changes that affect this space	Getting into the queue for connectivity – barriers?
Political ramifications and influence		Access to suppliers

These needs came from the question, "What do you need most to overcome the worry you voiced earlier?"

Target Audience Biggest Needs to Overcome their Worries		
Adopters	Attorneys	Company CEOs
Unbiased, fact-based information and education	Educated legislative groups at political level to drive the policy and regulators	Fact-based education (unbiased)
Advocacy—a voice to help navigate the political process	Public policy support—state, local, federal, and legal public policy	Advocacy to help my company plan properly. A team of advisors to approach policy makers
Assurance that my long-term investment is worth it	Constructive working relationships with other utilities to get my client's deals done	Working relationships with other companies in the industry to uncover future opportunity
Collaboration so I have choices for my utilities	Business leads / referral sources	Policy certainty and reinforcement

The preceding is ASEA's combined list of business worries and needs by member group. These were the combined responses to the questions: "What keeps you up at night? And what do you need most to overcome that worry?"

Assess what you see and find commonalities.

You now have a collection of worries and needs from your breakout groups. Each group presented their top five worries, followed by their top five needs. It is okay to clarify the need, but do not evaluate or rank the needs. To clarify the need is to ask, "Is this a 'nice to have'" or "Would it without a doubt help this member sleep better at night?" This is not the time to say, "I don't think that's a valid need" or "When I was in that member's shoes I didn't ever worry about that."

Distribute the list of common needs to all members and look for overlap. This is your sweet spot. If you can find two or three needs that two or three of the groups have in common, you are on the path to link up association benefits that are most relevant to your target member groups. If the need is consistent across groups, you will likely be offering a solution to a wider audience than your three target member groups.

If you cannot find at least a couple of member needs that overlap two or more member groups, you have more work to do. You will likely uncover *some* similar needs. If you are stuck, your volunteer leaders can add some perspective and can help fill in blanks and ask questions about needs that were not mentioned by the individual groups.

Do not add unsolicited member needs or distort their answers.

It is fine to question the responses, but discovery begins with your members' unedited input. If some of the common needs are beyond your association's control, remember that you do not exist to provide everything that a member needs in their work. There are some needs that you have no way to solve, are not part of your association's mission, or are not your responsibility to solve. If that is the case, you will simply disregard that need. Focus on worries and needs that you can overcome *today*. Your goal is to find three needs from across member groups that you can overcome through your offerings.

Step Two Action (part 3):

As a group, review the complete listing of needs by member group. Narrow them down to three common needs that your association can answer across your portfolio of services and offerings.

NOTE:

• This step is for the entire task force.
• Timing: two hours

Your Action Notes:

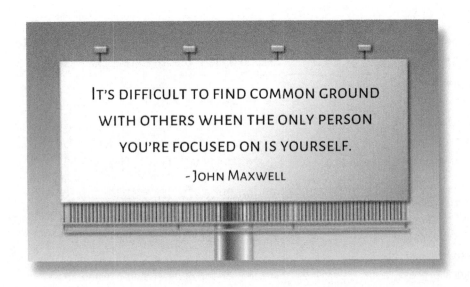

IT'S DIFFICULT TO FIND COMMON GROUND
WITH OTHERS WHEN THE ONLY PERSON
YOU'RE FOCUSED ON IS YOURSELF.

- JOHN MAXWELL

Step 3.
Link their needs with your expertise

Now is your chance to think about all the activities and services you do really well! You will link up the core strengths that you now know members need most with what you have the expertise to solve today. Focus on solutions *that answer their needs*. Your solutions that help your members sleep better at night will become your biggest strengths.

You might have a moment when you realize that long list of member benefits is no longer necessary to get your members' attention. Connect by solving one big need first, you then have the chance to expose them to all the other things you do that they do not think about daily.

As you complete this activity at the end of the chapter, refer to the ASEA's output for an example:

Biggest / Common member needs (from Steps 2 and 3)	What the Association does best to overcome/solve the need/problem (Association expertise)
Education/Information: • make complex topics simple, clear, honest • actively distribute objective, fact-based communications	• Data (from census), 3rd party research • Interconnectivity timelines • Conferences, newsletters, website for resources, fact sheets, policy updates
Advocacy/Public Policy work: • a voice to help navigate the political process, to help expand the market, champion the cause	• Distribute information above to supporters/supporting organizations • Centralized data that helps educate General Assembly and commission • Stay on top of new issues at General Assembly • Most accurate and timely information about state/federal decisions and new regulations
Constructive working relationships with stakeholders	• Behind the scenes work to find common ground • Meet, sit down and talk/listen to other providers and diverse industry competitors in spirit of opportunity

Trust (but verify) your expertise.

Take a look at the services and offerings that ASEA claim link up with the priority member needs in column two above. They were objective about: (1) what they claim they do well today, (2) the claim's alignment to their core mission, and (3) they distinguished their claim from other competitive sources. If you claim a category of expertise but do not deliver on it well today, the value message will not be credible.

Your association offerings will become the way you prove your claims. We call these the proof points in your value proposition.

As you review the list on the previous page, you may believe everything on the list of association expertise is something you do well today.

On the other hand, you might want to verify that your solution or offering is really that good. There are several possible approaches:

- Informal approach—validate with your task force: Uninvolved members of your task force are a good place to start to validate claims of value. Remind them to be open as you discuss the association competencies, share experience with your programs and services, and identify where they do not see value. Members will be honest. If they have not had experience with your programs, ask them if they would find your deliverables and offerings valuable.
- Formal approach—ask your members: If you survey members, create two kinds of questions: "How important are the following service/tools/offerings?" and "How satisfied are you with the services/tools/offerings?" Compare importance and satisfaction to verify if the solution you offer is equally important and useful. (List each service, tool, or offering in detail. Make sure the service is clear enough to give you the information you want to use.)
- Data-driven approach—conduct an internal program evaluation: An internal assessment complements member research. The simple process outlined in *Race for Relevance*, by co-authors Harrison Coerver and Mary Byers, can aide you in assessing products and services. I urge you to consider using this process as part of your strategic thinking, to validate your claims related to your value proposition. Combining this internal analysis with member research is the ideal, unbiased way to verify what you do effectively today. As the book describes, assign a score from one to five, with five as the highest for each of your key programs and services.

Program/ Service	Related-ness to Mission	Lifecycle Position	% of members that use	Financial Results/ Potential	Effective use of Staff/ Volunteer Time	Available from other Sources	Would we Start Today?	Total

Solving the uh-oh roadblock.

What if the value proposition discovery process uncovers *that members do not value the things we do well?* Or worse, *we cannot find anything that matches up* to what they say they need most?

In the spirit of questioning everything, welcome your task force's perspective to guide the process. This may be challenging when they focus on areas that differ from your view of your association's priorities or expertise.

When Marc Lebowitz, Association Executive at Ada County Association of REALTORS® (ACAR), began the value proposition process, he said, "We think we are enlightened and completely understand life in our members' world . . . but we don't. They see things that we can't and make connections that we don't think of."

I am thankful that *the long pause* actually happened at ACAR. The twenty members and staff around the table did not know what to say when they saw the combined list of what members need most. It was a humbling moment. But it led to a surprise. The connections were there, but the association did not see ACAR's offerings like the member did. President Kit had committed to "question everything." After a break and discussion, the group came back together and realized there were, in fact, four distinct needs that ACAR could answer that day.

The group transitioned from speechless to feeling driven to tackle new commitments. Thirty days after that workshop, Marc shared:

> We are now engaged in auditing our current service offerings to determine how we address the needs we promise in our value proposition. We will, without a doubt, be trimming out some of what we currently do and adding other things we have never thought of before. ACAR will build our programs around our new understanding about our members.

Step 3 Action: Make the Link

(1) List the common member needs you identified earlier down the left column of a two-column matrix.

(2) Brainstorm the specific activity, service, tool, or resource that you provide that answers each of the common needs and enter it into the second column of the matrix.

(3) If you cannot cite specific examples of how you satisfy the need today, leave it blank. (If you cannot substantiate your claim today, then it is not a credible solution.)

Take time out to clarify features and benefits.

This is a good opportunity to step back and define what we mean by linking up member needs with your expertise.

A common finding when reviewing association materials in any format, whether digital e-news, website landing pages, or hard copy materials, is heavy focus on features: classes, fundraising, tools, conference speaker. When a reader sees a class listing that simply mentions the speaker or cost, it misses sharing the real benefit, which is what the class will do to help the member be more successful, lower risk, or how to make his or her job easier. The best communicators connect the dots for their readers by calling out the resulting benefit.

Strong value propositions use proof points to present a category of features with a strong resulting benefit. A benefit that is sometimes tangible and less often emotional.

Here is a personal example to explain the difference between features and tangible and emotional benefits.

I almost exclusively fly Southwest Airlines in my work.

The feature is: I earn points towards A-List status every time I take a flight.

The tangible benefit is: the points I earn help me achieve A-list status, which allows me to automatically skip check-in, board early, and secure my favorite exit-row seat. All of these are beneficial but are not my core motivators for flying exclusively Southwest Airlines.

The emotional benefit rationalizes the one main reason I am loyal to Southwest. It helps me reconcile the worry about how much time I spend away from home for business travel.

When I board a plane, I know I am working towards something important to me and my family. Each December, I use my points for my family's airline tickets to fly all five of us to our vacation spot and spend uninterrupted time together.

The points are merely a feature. What I can do as a result of earning those points is the emotional benefit. Emotional benefits help overcome a worry or satisfy a significant need. They are a strong motivator for my loyalty and my predisposition to Southwest Airlines.

When an association can help members move ahead in their career, lower their risk, or learn something that takes them to the next level in their business, the rationale moves from tangible to the emotional benefits of membership. This is a strong tool to help you get more of your members' attention.

Feature	Benefit
Has Rational Relevance	Has Emotional Relevance
A Label	Solves a Problem
Descriptive	Relieves a Worry
Tangible	Intangible
Examples:	Examples:
"Free tech webinar"	"Helps me balance my business/personal life."
"Our conference will have over 100 speakers"	"New knowledge boosts my confidence."
"24-hour legal help line"	"Lowers my risk."

You're halfway through the process!

You collected some insanely honest
and valuable information.

You're on the cusp of something relevant and one-of-a-kind!

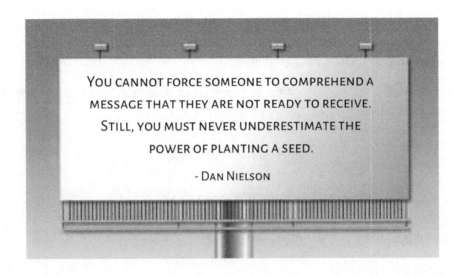

YOU CANNOT FORCE SOMEONE TO COMPREHEND A MESSAGE THAT THEY ARE NOT READY TO RECEIVE. STILL, YOU MUST NEVER UNDERESTIMATE THE POWER OF PLANTING A SEED.

- DAN NIELSON

Step 4.
Compose your proof points and draft your theme

A proof point is a phrase or sentence that describes how you answer one of the needs you identified in Step 3. Again, it's often expressed as a feature plus a benefit. You will craft one proof point to summarize how you respond to each need you decide to address.

Let us use ASEA to explain how to clarify this step. One common need members identified was getting valid, up-to-date, and unbiased information. The association believed they excelled at this.

Use the association's expertise identified in Step 3 to brainstorm a phrase that summarizes how you answer the member need for valid, up-to-date, and unbiased information.

Information is what ASEA offers, but instead of saying "we provide education and information," which is a tangible offering, they moved beyond the feature of information and offered the emotional benefit: the information gives members the ability to "make sense of complex issues." This is something that helps overcome the members' worry about being current on policy changes that affect this space. It also answers members' concern about political ramifications around sustainable energy.

Member's biggest needs	What the Association does best	Proof Points
Education/Information: make complex topics simple, clear, honest; actively distribute objective, fact-based communications	• Data (from census), 3rd party research • Interconnectivity timelines • Conferences, newsletters, website for resources, fact sheets, policy updates	1. Make sense of complex issues in the energy arena
Advocacy/Public Policy: a voice to help navigate the political process, to help expand the market, champion the cause	• Distribute information above to supporters/supporting organizations • Centralized data that helps educate General Assembly and commission • Stay on top of new issues at General Assembly • Most accurate and timely information about state/federal decisions and new regulations	2. Navigate the political process to champion the cause
Constructive working relationships with stakeholders	• Behind the scenes work to find common ground • Meet, sit down and talk/listen to other providers and diverse industry competitors in spirit of opportunity	3. Build constructive relationships to advance mutual interests between the public sector and the consumer

Breakthrough Value

The phrase for each category of benefits shows the way the organization proves their claim. For ASEA, you can see in the chart at the left how the link to member needs became three ways they prove their claim of value. These are called proof points.

Do the same exercise for each of the common needs from step 3. Each will have its own proof point.

Keep the words simple so your audience can remember them.

Simple and clear words are signs of a strong value proposition.

There are some universal standards for effective writing. Some of the most well-known are to focus more on your reader than you do on yourself. Another standard from the American Readership Institute finds that short sentences with fewer than fourteen words yield significantly higher comprehension than longer ones. And finally, language that is clear, simple, and scannable is more likely to get attention.

Beware of common pitfalls.

Developing proof points is the step where associations can take a wrong turn. They convince themselves that the tangible benefits (the proof points) are all that matter. Now that you validated what members most need your job is over, right? Wrong. It is not over until you develop your theme.

In addition, resist the temptation to only offer up needs that the leaders think are important. If you insert leaders' thinking at this point, you no longer have a member value proposition; you will have a leader value proposition!

Additional advice for this essential step.

- Give your ideas time to marinade but keep your momentum.

- Stay focused on the needs you compiled in step 2. Do not add or invent any needs in this step.

Narrow in on a theme that sells your solution.

With your three or four proof points in front of you, now you will brainstorm the main solution and your promise! You are looking for the emotional solution you offer your worried members to help them sleep better at night. The theme is the hook that tells your story. Let me explain what I mean by a hook with an analogy.

In music, a hook is a key ingredient of any song. Think for a minute about Marvin Gaye and Tammi Terrell's rendition of "Ain't No Mountain High Enough," by husband and wife team Nickolas Ashford and Valerie Simpson. A hook is a few relatable words, in this case the chorus that touches something in the audience's lives that makes the world seem smaller and more manageable. The words in the chorus repeat and stick in your mind, bringing you back to the premise in the song. Each time the hook connects you closer to the words.

Returning to our example, ASEA first prioritized three tangible ways the association delivers on their members' biggest common needs. Next, they brainstormed possible over-arching themes, and then narrowed to a short list of key phrases. This short list of phrases will be potential value messages. They all offer an emotional rationale for why the member should belong (or why someone should join.)

Here are the five value proposition theme ideas developed by ASEA, each with a different angle:

- Working for the future of energy in <geographic area> for all stakeholders.
- A clean ecosystem for the good of <geographic area>.
- A [realistic/accurate/up to date] roadmap to reach your objectives.
- We put our energy where your interests are.
- We take sides. We are on your side.

This was an exercise in free thinking—the group let their mind make connections to new ideas. It took more than one meeting to brainstorm a list of ideas that they considered viable theme options.

Once they had a collection of possible themes, the task force came to consensus on one theme about which the team could get inspired.

In our association example, the ASEA task force chose the theme *We Put Our Energy Where Your Interests Are* as the foundation of their value proposition.

Once the task force chose the theme, it was time to test it. Did the message resonate with each member of the task force? It did, even if several of the members were not part of the three target member groups. Remember this step requires consensus

Breakthrough Value

building, so it may not be each person's top choice, but the process helped to ensure that the theme choices related to common needs across all three target member groups.

If the message does not resonate with each member of the task force, take time to discuss it and tweak the message as you need to.

From the overall theme, they next developed additional copy to explain the message, position the proof points, and layout a rationale they were happy with.

What follows is ASEA's words that make up their value proposition. It combines a theme (to resonate with the reader), proof points (to differentiate and substantiate how ASEA is unique), and a call to action (to encourage the member or prospect to learn more). These are only the words. The next step is to put it into a picture for promotion.

While I resist making generalizations in conducting value proposition projects, I have observed that while no two member groups are exactly the same, many member groups do share a few core business needs. While one single message will not resonate with every member equally, you can select a successful theme for significant groups of members when you spend some dedicated time listening and getting to know them.

The value message, as stated earlier, should be as relevant to a prospect as it is to a current member. A value message cannot do the heavy lifting to convince someone to join, but it should be convincing enough to plant a seed and lead the prospect to a live person who can close the deal.

We put our energy into building a sustainable environment to support your interests and the best possible future for all stakeholders. Let's partner to: ◄ THEME

· Make sense of complex issues in the energy arena

· Navigate the political process to champion the cause ◄ 3 PROOF POINTS

· Build constructive relationships to advance mutual interests between the public sector and the consumer.

Advancing your interests through collaboration, education, and influence. *When sustainability matters, we have the energy.*

Learn more at asea.org. ◄ CALL TO ACTION

Step 4 Action:

In part 1, compose the proof points that answer each of your small list of member needs. This can take one to two hours to complete.

Take a break and reconvene to finalize your proof points and move to part 2.

For part 2, brainstorm the emotional benefits that result from delivering on your three proof points. What problem does this solve? How will your solution make the member feel? How can you best relate to them to get their attention?

Note:

The entire task force and the communications staff will take this next step together.

It will take two different meetings to complete this step.

Your Action Notes:

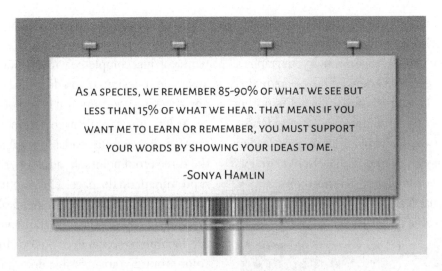

As a species, we remember 85-90% of what we see but less than 15% of what we hear. That means if you want me to learn or remember, you must support your words by showing your ideas to me.

-Sonya Hamlin

Step 5.
Complement your words with graphics

Once you complete the initial theme ideas, take a break for at least a day or two and reconvene to choose the theme and finalize your message. Then, once your message is final, it is time to develop a picture to tell the story. Capture member interest with more than words, and connect them visually.

Sonya Hamlin, in her book *How to Talk So People Listen*, says that, "as a species, we remember 85-90% of what we see but less than 15% of what we hear. That means if you want me to learn or remember, you must support your words by showing your ideas to me."

Most of your readers are "scanners" and "flippers." They do not read every word. Let graphics help tell your story to pull the reader in and capture the scanner's attention. Simply put, the member's brain likes pictures.

This is the chance to show your association's personality. Yes, its personality is one of the best ways your association can set itself apart from others. The competition cannot copy your association's unique personality. This is your chance to share your personality and relay your new message through your graphics.

If you have ever experienced how personality can help create lasting relationships with another person, the process of building a business identity works the same way. I have heard association leaders express that they are "professional but not stodgy," or, one of my favorites, "more a Prius than a BMW."

These attributes can guide your voice and display the story your value proposition conveys.

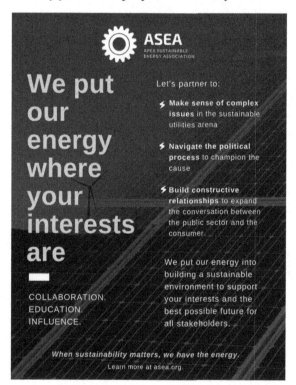

I suggest you make an investment in a professional layout for your message. Do not sacrifice the work you just completed with so much care by using an amateur design. If you do not have in-house talent, there is a good amount of remote talent online.

At left, our sample association conveyed their message in a simple, readable graphic that calls out the three proof points. In addition, the main theme is prominent on the page. The graphic is clear about how the association delivers their solution.

Caution: Do not assume that a visually appealing document is enough ... but putting imagery and color around your message does a lot to tell your value story and get attention. Get the words right first. Then tell the story through graphics and color to capture attention.

Step 5 Action: Stop to consider the personality you want to convey to your audience.

Is your brand:

Professional? Inspirational? Academic? Casual? Nurturing?

Turn your words into a picture.

Developing the graphics will involve a designer who can give you at least three design choices. Then work together to finalize the materials. This will likely take a minimum of two weeks.

Step 6.
Develop your launch plan

Your goal is to expose every member to your value message. That includes the three groups you resourced in step 1, as well as the broader membership. Take advantage of this time to think through how your association will present the new value proposition message to better brand your association with previously uninterested, new, and prospective members.

To set the stage for this step, here is my favorite Harry Beckwith story from his book *Selling the Invisible*:

Driving down the freeway you switch on your radio station and hear a song for the first time. You like it but don't remember it. The next afternoon you hear the song again. Perhaps you note the singer and perhaps you remember her name. Two mornings later you hear the song again. After making sure no other commuters are watching you start to sing along with the hook, which you now remember. Two days later you buy the CD (or today you would download off Spotify). You play it several times. By the third evening you know most of the words. It has taken seven or eight playings for the song's message to sink in. But finally, it has. What if the singer changed the song and tune every time? What would you remember? Almost nothing.

Now apply that to a rationale, or a key message for why a member should belong? What does this tell you about your messaging strategy? Can you keep changing your words, your melody, your theme and your words? If you do, what will people remember? For what will they know you? After you say one thing, repeat it again and again and again.

You have a new way to present yourself to be memorable. How will you plan, promote, launch, and use this new value message across platforms to reach your many different audiences?

Plan for your value proposition reveal.

Once the launch plan is complete, it becomes part of your bigger communications plan. Think about your value proposition launch as a splash—like a political campaign—not a drip campaign that you trickle out a little at a time. A splash helps you to get distracted members' attention.

Do not underestimate the value of a thought-out plan to help you organize yourself, your communications staff, and your spokespeople.

You have a new engaging message to share, but it will not sell itself. Get organized before you launch.

- Where will you promote your new message?
- Who do you most want to influence?
- How will you present the message to key member groups?
- What material can help you reinforce the message and raise awareness with all members?

Here are ten possible actions to get your mind into brainstorming how to integrate your value proposition into your launch materials:

1. *About Us Page*: a fresh landing page on your website with a compelling explanation of "what we deliver to you"
2. *Prospecting Materials*: brochures, fliers, or postcards that are suitable for handing out through direct or electronic mail
3. *Graphics Library*: repository of graphics for web, promotions, and digital use
4. *Printed Promotional Media*: banners and posters to display in your lobby and classrooms and at events and meetings

5. *Installations and Event Giveaways*: items that members may take away to remember and help spread the message
6. *Talking Points*: one-page references for your leaders to use for keynote addresses, smaller member meetings, and one-on-one interactions
7. *Website*: incorporate your new value message as inspiration for a web refresh or a new slider on the homepage
8. *Annual Report*: report results of the process to the membership and raise awareness of the association's most relevant member benefits that reinforce the value proposition
9. *Association Voicemail Recording*: incorporate into your phone system as a first contact with callers as a reminder of what they should expect from you
10. *Video*: messages from a staff executive, board president or chair that invite the member to reset or validate their impression of your association

> **Step 6 Action**: Document your launch plan in a matrix or spreadsheet format for easy reference.
>
> The launch plan is a communications staff responsibility. It might take a week or two to draft, collaborate with the Association Executive, and finalize.

Feed and guide your communications plan.

Karl Berron, the CEO of the Indiana Association of REALTORS®, expressed why it was important to get an outside set of eyes on their communications plan. In his words:

> We need a thought-out approach to integrating our value proposition into our daily activities, and the discipline to execute it. Staff training and buy-in is part of it, as is a comprehensive plan for delivering the message.

You are now ready to integrate your new message into your master communication plan.

- *Editorial Strategy*: You have the framework to develop editorial around your proof points to reinforce and build upon your expertise.
- *Content Strategy*: You can begin to build out your proof points with more detail for each. Offer examples, in-depth articles and blog posts, and testimonials as part of the strategy to help members learn how your expertise helps other members.

In the rush of the day, a thought-out plan helps you remember that your value proposition is the foundation of your communication plan. A plan is also the best way to think through how to get staff and leaders comfortable with their role as your brand ambassadors.

Position benefits outside of the value proposition.

Events are likely not part of your formal value message . . . that said, the theme, the speakers, and the topics presented at those events should align closely with your value proposition (delivering on what your members need most). The more you place your value proposition at the front of your mind, the more you will look for, and plan for, a tie-in.

If your value message revolves around *protection*, it might be a challenge to link anything beyond advocacy in your content strategy. Think again. The better you get to know and use the message, the more skilled you will become at finding new ways to present an expanded angle to the idea of protection. For example, gaining education is an important way to protect members from making costly mistakes. Volunteer opportunities are another way for members to actively protect their industry.

If a service or tool or resource does not fit, it might be time to reevaluate it. It can be difficult to let go of decisions made a long time ago by an influential person or group of people, or that could impact staff.

This is your chance to question everything with a clean slate to discuss a future direction. The decision could be as simple as an operational change, or it might be part of strategic thinking about the future of your organization.

Your value proposition is the enticement that brings the member into your organization, providing the chance to tell them about other offerings that can help them be better at what they do.

So, if an important member benefit is part of your mission but does not exactly fit inside your value proposition, it is fine to explain those offerings as:

- *other services as you need them,*
- *additional resources when you are in a bind, or*
- *other tools to ensure <a benefit outside your value message>.*

And again, it might be time to contemplate if it belongs in your portfolio at all.

Get your staff on board.

While all staff and leaders are the ambassadors for the new message, the communications director is key to incorporating the message throughout all member communications. Once your message is final, present it to your staff and spend some time to brief them on the value proposition, to get their head around the new theme, and encourage them to begin to use it before the launch.

In a formal meeting, ask your staff for their ideas for possible ways to use your value proposition in communications and interactions with members. Association executives report that the value proposition process boosts staff morale, as well as member understanding. Staff are responsible to deliver your new promise of value to members in everyday interactions and are the carriers of your value message, so give them tools to show value. The best way is for them to learn from each other. You should find that this new approach gives staff a feeling of pride and accomplishment in having a message to use in their member dealings.

Recognize and reward good use of the message when you see it—talk about it in staff meetings and live it consistently. I have seen association staff have fun brainstorming the craziest ideas for a successful launch and for keeping the message in front of members. Two of my favorite promotional tactics to launch a new value proposition are:

1. a homepage graphic of an airplane banner carrying the message
2. a fortune cookie stuffed with the value message as a takeaway from an all-member meeting

Encourage your staff to experiment and talk about their experiences. This maximizes staff comfort when they might not know how to put the value proposition into their own words. In addition, do not neglect to brief every new staff member on the association's value proposition during your onboarding process.

Step 7.
Launch

Once your people are prepped and your plan and your materials are ready, it is time to launch the new message. To get here, you have accomplished a great deal.

- Your leaders are prepped
- Your staff are comfortable in their roles
- Signs are made and the website is updated
- Postcards are in the mail

- Staff email signature blocks are updated
- New member materials are ready

Choose a milestone to launch your new promise—an installation meeting of the new board of directors, an all-member meeting, in preparation for dues renewal season, or even at the beginning of a new year.

Think through a time that you will get a good amount of member attention. You invested a lot in getting ready for this moment. You are ready: so go!

Consider Carol Platt's reflections from OSCAR's launch. Carol chose to use the value proposition announcement during a key moment: the summer months through outreach to prospective members and outreach to members prior to dues renewal. Carol said:

> I sent the (value proposition) postcard to both existing members and our database of non-members. Feedback was immediate in contacts from non-members, and we had more renewals come in earlier than ever before. Coincidence, perhaps, but I don't think so.

Part 3:

Preparation to Repetition to Payoff

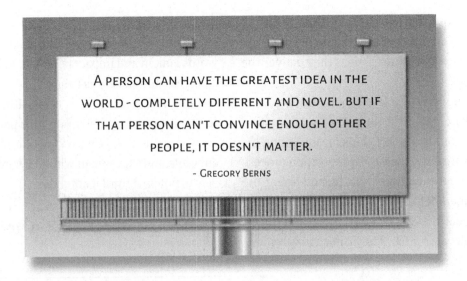

A PERSON CAN HAVE THE GREATEST IDEA IN THE WORLD - COMPLETELY DIFFERENT AND NOVEL. BUT IF THAT PERSON CAN'T CONVINCE ENOUGH OTHER PEOPLE, IT DOESN'T MATTER.

- GREGORY BERNS

Equip your leaders and staff to sell the new message

I learned a concept in my early-management career at Xerox called "managing up" from a mentor, Duane Lock.

Managing people is more than doing what you think is right to get the job done. Managing is doing what will help your team (and your boss or the leader) get their jobs done, too. In other words, this under-acknowledged management philosophy is the idea that if you give your boss or your team your full support and then the spotlight, it is as important as anything you can do as a leader.

If you want to help your board president succeed and your directors be confident with the message, help them learn to sell the message. By developing the value proposition, you enable them with credible material for an effective all-member meeting or a one-on-one conversation. With the right motivation, reinforcement, and practice, the new message will inspire them as they deliver the new message.

Every year when new leaders join the board, ask your president to take the time at board orientation to back brief on the project. This means taking his or her peers through the value proposition process backstory, what the project solved, and orient the new board members to the message. This will help keep your board-level sales force fresh and united with their elevator pitch. They can customize it as they see fit.

Lorin Woolfe, in *The Bible on Leadership*, says:

Leadership takes an almost bottomless supply of verbal energy: working the phones, staying focused on your message, repeating the same mantra until you can't stand the sound of your own voice—and then repeating it some more, because just when you start to become bored 'witless' with the message, it's probably starting to seep into the organization.

You may seem like a broken record, reminding your leaders how important it is to repeat the new message all the time, over and over again, with every interaction or opportunity to share it with members and non-members alike. But, when your message becomes part of the way you lead, you will see words sink in and impact behavior. When behavior changes, culture begins to shift.

Your new message will seem a little rigid at first. It is just words until you put your personality and creativity into it. Live with it awhile, say it in different ways, and experiment with the words. This is the way to polish it until it shines.

Regroup and reflect on your progress.

Action:

On page 22, you asked your Board or Executive Committee to answer that question about the single most important benefit that (1) your association does best that (2) your members need most. Now it's time to take out those index cards so that each person who responded can see the difference in the way they answered the question before you started the project. The before-after comparison touches each person directly to see their words next to the new message that everyone will use going forward.

Here is an example of an association executive's answer to the question, before they discovered their value proposition:

Membership with us has a direct impact on a member's business success and their financial bottom line through the legal, tech, and information resources their membership gives them access to. Membership opens the door to networking and business opportunities with peers who are committed to high standards of ethics and professionalism in our industry.

It is not uncommon that the response is more than one single benefit and focuses on tangible services, in other words, the features that the association offers. Sometimes intangible member benefits are part of the mix, like "protecting business interests" or "upholding high standards of ethics and professionalism." After the value proposition was complete, the CEO had a new elevator pitch to express the value of the association:

Our members actively participate in protecting their own business interests, the interests of the industry, and the property rights of all property owners across our state.

For this association, members helped to rediscover that the biggest emotional benefit across their three different member groups led to the theme:

Arming You with Answers. One overarching message with several implied ways the association delivers on the promise to protect the member's business. The theme now speaks to the facts and the feelings that the association wants the member to remember.

Practice your elevator pitch.

Your theme will help everyone remember the message. Do not fear that you are overdoing it—remember that, to be memorable, you will need to be consistent and repeat the theme in different ways, through different media, and in unique methods based on the audience.

Soon it will sink in and become a second-nature way you answer the "what's in it for the member" question every time, in all kinds of interactions.

You can set a great example for leaders and staff when you champion your value proposition. Challenge them to advocate for your value proposition as naturally as you advocate for the latest issue at the Capitol.

After you champion the effort with your interpretation of the message, give leaders the skills *they* need to be your extended sales force. It might not come naturally to them. This means teaching them how to relay the value message in one-on-one interactions, business owner/CEO presentations, or at an all-member event like an installation. Give them a structure for their presentation and help them build credibility through practice. Yes, give them the opportunity to practice on camera so they will be effective advocates for the new message.

Here are two methods to help your leaders grow more comfortable with the message:

1. A board (or executive team) and key senior staff member workshop to review the value proposition and receive training on how to deliver the value message to any member group. Successful sessions include asking every participant to develop a three-minute presentation (in their own words) and present the value proposition as if they were in front of a group of new members. They practice in front of each other to see the different ways in which each person articulates the message.
2. An association president and the association CEO travel to business-owner offices to pay a thank-you visit, during which they explain what the association means to a business owner in clear and simple terms, and share a printed brochure that highlights the value proposition. The discussion, questions, and conversation build from there.

Keep your message alive through practice. Verify that board members understand the message. Then,

inform and prepare your new leaders every year. They will need exposure to what a value proposition is, how you developed yours, and how they are expected to use it to represent the association.

How does an organization deliver on a promise so well that someone can actually feel it?

Years ago, I read a book while sitting in the waiting room at Mayo Clinic where our daughter was a patient. Between appointments, we walked into a bookstore where I saw the book *Management Lessons from Mayo Clinic*, written by Leonard Berry and Kent Seltman. The title caught my attention because I had recently launched nSight Marketing and was in my studying and observation phase to test some of my own ideas.

To me, Mayo Clinic was a complete marketing and brand phenomenon. Not only did their brand suggest credibility and a systematic process before we arrived, but Mayo Clinic knew exactly how to

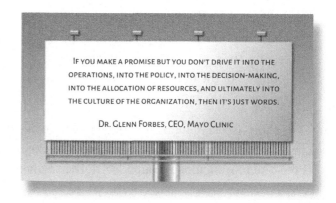

IF YOU MAKE A PROMISE BUT YOU DON'T DRIVE IT INTO THE OPERATIONS, INTO THE POLICY, INTO THE DECISION-MAKING, INTO THE ALLOCATION OF RESOURCES, AND ULTIMATELY INTO THE CULTURE OF THE ORGANIZATION, THEN IT'S JUST WORDS.

DR. GLENN FORBES, CEO, MAYO CLINIC

deliver on their promise. When they say *the patient comes first*, they not only promote the promise, but they also delivered on it in real-time by calling our daughter within five minutes of sitting down in the reception area for every one of her dozen appointments that spanned two days. The doctors showed their commitment to the patient through investing in technology that allowed every doctor to see results from exams or tests prior to us walking into the exam room. We felt like our daughter was valued. Our time was valued. We could tell that they delivered on their promise that she came first. We could feel their promise in every interaction across the medical center.

Action: Consider the various ways that you can help leaders and staff convey and live your new value proposition to a variety of member groups and situations.

Your Action Notes:

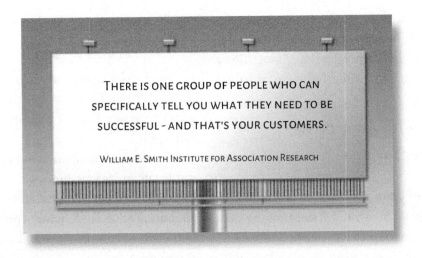

THERE IS ONE GROUP OF PEOPLE WHO CAN SPECIFICALLY TELL YOU WHAT THEY NEED TO BE SUCCESSFUL - AND THAT'S YOUR CUSTOMERS.

WILLIAM E. SMITH INSTITUTE FOR ASSOCIATION RESEARCH

Trust, and then verify, the message gets through

Conventional wisdom, the business environment, and global market conditions change all the time. So, you must have a way to verify that the worries you respond to today will still be relevant next year.

Member needs shift with the industry, economy, market (locally or beyond), changes in competition, stage of a member's career, changes in their life outside work, and even external, uncontrollable events.

What members worry about today might not work in two, three, or five years.

Needs could change abruptly during a crisis. When COVID-19 struck in 2020, members immediately understood the power of an association that advocates successfully for an industry to qualify as an essential service or to organize grassroots calls to action for a new regulation that could impact the industry. For some time to come, members will see first-hand how the benefit of political and also community affairs can unify a membership. Associations are making the critical transition from virus to value.

Be patient with your post-launch expectations.

Frankly, many of your members are probably not paying that much attention. It will take time to reach them and for them to consider your new rationale. Some will say *aha* right away, while others will slowly begin to notice a change in the way you communicate and deliver on your services. And frankly, there may be a group of members (outside of and possibly within your target member groups) who never connect with your new message.

Launching a new message strategy is a learning process that takes time. Ron Heifetz, author of *Perspectives on Change*, explains the difference between a technical challenge and an adaptive one:

> The technical is defined as those that can be solved by the knowledge of experts, whereas adaptive requires new learning. When the problem, definition, solution, and implementation is clear.... For the adaptive, change must come from the collective intelligence of the employees at all levels.

So, together they learn their way toward solutions."

You cannot change a customer's mind immediately. They will see or hear the words, but until they experience your promise in action, they may not "get it."

In addition, members will not see a difference until staff and leadership begin to show and speak in a unified mantra. Your staff is the front line for communicating and living your value proposition. This cannot be the job for solely your chief communicator.

There are several ways to trust, but verify, that your value proposition is making its way through to your members and stays relevant to your most important member groups:

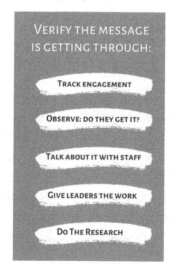

VERIFY THE MESSAGE IS GETTING THROUGH:

TRACK ENGAGEMENT

OBSERVE: DO THEY GET IT?

TALK ABOUT IT WITH STAFF

GIVE LEADERS THE WORK

DO THE RESEARCH

- *Look for growth in participation and engagement.* When members recognize what they get, they will be more willing to check out what else you have to offer them, to raise their hand to learn more, or self-initiate getting involved!
- *Keep your eyes open.* How do new members receive the explanation of the value proposition the first time they walk in the door? Do they seem to understand?
- *Talk about progress.* Your board members have a pulse on what members are saying out there. Take time in board meetings to discuss how members talk about the association. Ask the board to explain how they relay the value proposition when they interact with members and how members respond.
- *Do a little reconnaissance work with the intent to find promising conversations.* Send an outsider to your office to pose as a prospective new member. Request that they ask a question like, "What can I expect from your association?" In front of the entire staff, give ample recognition to staff who use their own words to explain a simple, overarching answer about the value of membership that includes the key parts of the value proposition.
- *Conduct regular member research.* Make a commitment to survey your membership every year. During your annual survey of members, include the question, "How satisfied are you with the value you receive from <your association>?" Pay attention to the percent of responses indicating strong satisfaction. Compare year-over-year differences in the very satisfied rating. Celebrate your progress and analyze any challenges that should be addressed.
- *Give leaders and staff the work.* Continue to motivate your leaders and board to get back on track if you have not been consistent. Solicit from them new ways to articulate your value proposition. Just as your expertise differs from your association neighbor or a competing association, your leaders and staff will have unique ideas about how to articulate your association's value proposition.

A new message will inspire new strategies

If you have seen your message come alive through the words of your leaders and staff, you will appreciate the power of a unified rationale. Like a lighthouse or a beacon, an intentional message gives an organization a clear target for which to aim. And the message can alter the trajectory of the association.

I had the chance to work with the leadership of Baldwin REALTORS® in developing their strategic plan, followed by developing their value proposition. After both were well underway, I complimented CEO Sheila Dodson for how she guided her leadership team to focus on that beacon which read: *To be the most sought-after association whose members are the most elite professionals in the region.* Sheila confidently, yet humbly, responded, "It isn't from anything I did. My board is laser-focused on our vision. They want the REALTOR® image, and their vision, to mean something."

Theirs was a firm commitment, different from what I have ever seen from a leadership team—and it was the result of a CEO and board of directors who were equally committed, from vision to action.

Today, they continue to have an equally strong commitment to keeping their value proposition alive.

Deliver on your promise every day.

I will bet you and your leaders know enough about marketing to know that backing up your claims of expertise with action (and a plan) continually strengthens your promise. In other words, strengthen *the right* strengths.

For example, if your association is really good at providing solutions to technology issues to stay ahead of change, then live it. Master and deliver current solutions with absolute expertise and be the visionary for what comes next, especially considering the continuing pace of change in technology today. Make strategic decisions and associated investments in new offerings to strengthen the promise of what you do well.

This is a stepping-off point for your organization to re-evaluate all your programs through the lens of your new value proposition. You can then use this process to make strategic decisions about where, how, and when to invest your resources, knowing your decisions are rooted in the real experiences of your members.

Anne Marie Matteo, CEO from Suburban West REALTORS® Association, offered thoughtful reflection years after developing their value proposition:

The value proposition brings us back home. It reminds us of our core beliefs and motivates us to master these tenets. We also incorporate the value proposition into our strategic plan to strengthen our focus to be mindful of the priorities we promised.

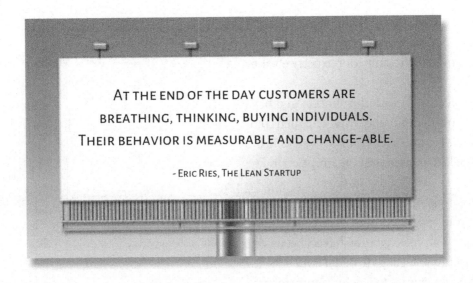

AT THE END OF THE DAY CUSTOMERS ARE
BREATHING, THINKING, BUYING INDIVIDUALS.
THEIR BEHAVIOR IS MEASURABLE AND CHANGE-ABLE.

- ERIC RIES, THE LEAN STARTUP

Final Notes

When this process is complete, I hope you realize that changing members' perceptions of your association is no mystery at all. By following a plan, and respecting a proven process, you will gain much more than a message in the end. Internally, your association will establish more confidence, unity, and credibility, knowing you are all focusing on one fundamental emotional benefit of belonging, in addition to all the tangible benefits that support the message. This is breakthrough value! Externally,

you have the chance to persuade your members to pay attention. Prepare to hear unsolicited comments like one young professional in Pennsylvania who encountered her association's newly-launched value proposition and remarked, "Something's changed. I am clearer about what I should expect from my association. I even feel like I want to get involved."

Remember: no two value propositions are alike. Yours is like a fingerprint, it is yours alone. There is no one-size-fits-all list of what members need most or what you do best. Your members are different from anyone else, the member groups you choose to target are yours alone, and your expertise varies by association.

If you are persistent with this process and have the determination to find your "why" and then communicate it with confidence, you will overcome the biggest obstacle that faces your organization today: indifference.

Congratulations! I hope you have a new way to think about your association and its strengths. Now that you know your message, you have all you need to combine facts and feelings to better connect with the people you most want to reach: your members.

Perhaps *you* just found *your* money moment!

Project Plan — Key activities to reference as you work through the process

Part 1 – Pre-plan

☐ A. Agree on what this project will solve - page 21
☐ B. Get ready. Assemble your task force – page 25

Part 2 – Seven Steps

☐ 1. Select target member groups. Brainstorm and prioritize two or three member groups most important to your association's success – page 34
☐ 2. Listen to their worries and prioritize their needs – page 37
☐ 3. Link their needs to your expertise - page 44
☐ 4. Compose proof points, and then draft and finalize your theme - page 54
☐ 5. Develop graphics to turn your words into a picture. Finalize your message and graphics - page 56
☐ 6. Develop your launch plan – page 59

☐ 7. Value proposition launch – page 63

Part 3 – Preparation to Repetition to Payoff

☐ C. Practice the pitch - equip your leaders to sell the new message - page 68
☐ D. Discuss how to tailor by situation and identify staff best practices – page 71
☐ E. Prepare for the launch – president or CEO announcement – pages 68-70
☐ F. Use new messages in all member interactions – page 63
☐ G. Verify annually that the message is getting through – page 75
☐ H. Review the message annually with new leaders and staff– page 68

Value Proposition Project Plan

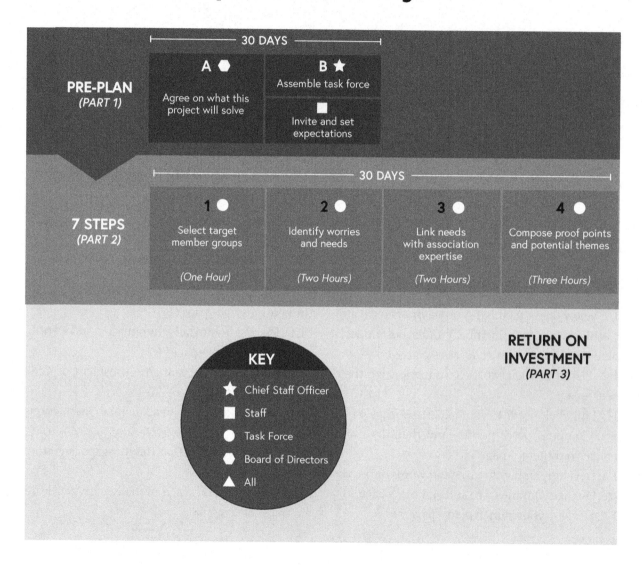

PRE-PLAN
(PART 1)

30 DAYS

A ⬡
Agree on what this project will solve

B ★
Assemble task force

◼
Invite and set expectations

7 STEPS
(PART 2)

30 DAYS

1 ●
Select target member groups

(One Hour)

2 ●
Identify worries and needs

(Two Hours)

3 ●
Link needs with association expertise

(Two Hours)

4 ●
Compose proof points and potential themes

(Three Hours)

RETURN ON INVESTMENT
(PART 3)

KEY

★ Chief Staff Officer

◼ Staff

● Task Force

⬡ Board of Directors

▲ All

This chart sets expectations for the timing and role of the many people who will be part of the process. Each section relates to the three sections in the book. It provides a suggested timeline, who is responsible for each step, and the dependencies between association groups to successfully complete the project.

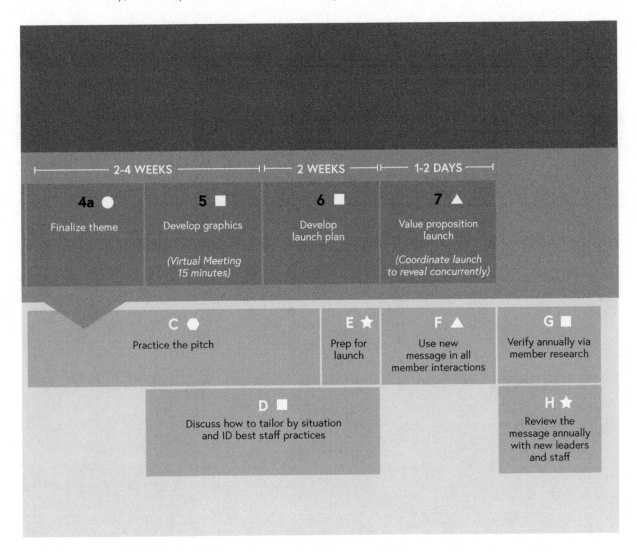

Acknowledgements

If not for COVID-19, this book would not be in your hands today. Similarly, if not for my family, friends and colleagues in personal and professional circles, I would not have the chance to experiment with the many lessons and practices I use today. I am a human repository of their stories, teachings, advice, and inspiration.

- Thanks to the many association executives who offered me the chance to help question the ideas in this book through their experiences using this process. Their advice and collaboration allowed me to continually improve the seven-step process. Every project solidified the approach, but my special thanks go out to:
Karl Berron (CEO, IAR)
Andrea Bowles (Blanchard and Calhoun, GA)
Laura Crowther (CEO, CCAR)
Sheila Dodson (CEO, Baldwin REALTORS®)
Kit Fitzgerald (Past President, ACAR)
Suzan Koren (former CEO, REALSource)
Marc Lebowitz (former CEO, ACAR)
Anne Marie Matteo (CEO, SWRA)
Michael Readinger (CEO, CHHSM)

- I owe an enormous debt of gratitude to association colleagues who read this book in its early form and gave me detailed and constructive feedback, including: Veronica Precella, Roger Turcotte, Carol Platt, and Randy Steinman.

- I am grateful to these corporate teachers, supporters, and friends who influenced the concepts in this book and the way I think about the work:

Amos Gallaway taught me the value of a process-driven and a relationship-based business. They can co-exist beautifully.

Ben Craig advised me, "When you make the transition (from corporate employee to entrepreneur), Go Like Hell!" He knew that a slow start makes for a slow growing business. The most successful value proposition launches follow this philosophy.

Al Purcell pushed me. His thinking was that when you expect the best in others, you usually get it. Communicate clear expectations, do not just hope that people will perform, and provide generous recognition when they do.

Duane Lock mentored me as I grew from being an individual contributor to a manager. He was teacher, challenger, and supporter wrapped into one. He encouraged me to verbalize my arguments and to challenge myself. I am forever thankful for his encouragement and counsel.

Melayne (Mel) Longwith crystallized the analogy of a value proposition so many years ago. She continues to live her promise.

Karen Gehle, CEO of Kansas Association of REALTORS® opened her doors to me and gave me my entré into the association world in 2007. I am indebted to her and KAR for the chance to learn, collaborate, and continue to work together today.

- The greatest gift for a small business is a talented team. I am thankful and proud of mine: Mike King, Teresa Mandala, Kelley Rodill, Carol Weinrich, and Ian Windsor. They supported the value proposition approach from inception through dozens of client projects. They each had a part in taking the value proposition approach from experiment to iteration, from launch to execution, to distribution of the finished product. With their support, we overcame our skepticism and verified that this was a repeatable and viable concept.

- Self-publishing was to me a foreign language, an unexpected and unique process. I hit nothing less than the jackpot to choose members of my new extended team in this journey. My editor, Jayme Gittings, for understanding enough about marketing to be a spot-on partner on this project and for her objective insight that gave me pause to question my assumptions. Teresa Mandala, for her talented, creative approach and cover design that tells our story, and to Mary Neighbour for her priceless advice through the challenging self-publishing process, as well as her seemingly effortless approach to layout design.

- Many years ago, I had a stroke of luck to welcome a seasoned marketing executive to nSight Marketing to share this journey. Kat Szymanski is a natural collaborator, communicator, and creator who has an eye on our vision. She believed in this book from the start and continually helps refine our approaches. Kat rides shotgun with me every day. She is a gift to my life, and a priceless member of our team.

- Joan Herman assured me that I didn't have to learn about, understand, or know how to spell copyright. My attorney and friend took all that off my plate, so I had one less thing to think about.

- My mother, Gerean, was the best communicator I ever knew. She had a way of spreading positive karma with her words, actions, thoughts, voicemails, a hug, and simply her presence (and smile). I always said to myself, "I don't want to grow up to be like my mom—who can compete with that?" Today, I think of her and say to myself, "If only I could be a little more like my mother!"

- Jessie and Spencer Sight teach me every day that there is nothing more valuable than being genuine—to be an individual and live life in their own exceptional way. Watching them grow up into their best selves has been the most meaningful gift in my life. They helped me grow into a parent and a better communicator through our shared experiences. Ours is a beautiful, priceless journey.

- If not for Dan Sight, I might well still be a quiet, middle child who carried a lot of ideas and opinions inside. He taught me and encourages me every day to communicate even when it's hard to do. He taught me that little gets resolved if you hold your thoughts inside. However hard it can be to engage in courageous and respectful conversations, it's the only way to live our most authentic life. He effortlessly shows me every day that strong relationships are built through communication, consistency, common courtesy, and a sense of humor. It brings me so much joy to have him by my side through our journey. As a native Kansan, I fully endorse the feeling that Dorothy coined, from the *Wizard of Oz*: "There's no place like home."

Attributions

I suspect each of these authors have sat in their own quiet place to evaluate their personal philosophies and experiences, and then study, evaluate, and distill wisdom from others. I was influenced by people who shared their insights with me. With thanks and appreciation, I would like to acknowledge the following authors, publications, and organizations who inspire me:

American Readership Institute
Beckwith, Harry - Selling the Invisible, 1997, 2014
Berry, Leonard and Seltman, Kent - Management Lessons from Mayo Clinic, 2008
Hoffman, Bryce, Red Teaming, 2017
Coerver, Harrison and Byers, Mary - Race for Relevance, 2011
Goodman, Michael A. - The Marketing Guru
Hamlin, Sonya - How to Talk So People Listen, 1988
Heifetz, Ron - The Practice of Adaptive Leadership: Tools and Tactics for Changing Your Organization and the World, 2009
Heifetz, Ron - Leading Adaptive Change, 2014
Langhans, Terri - The 7 Marketing Mistakes Every Business Makes, 2003
Maxwell, John - Everyone Communicates, Few Connect, 2010
Ries, Eric - The Lean Startup, 2011

Slater, Jeffrey - Marketing Sage
Vinjamuri, David - Accidental Branding: How Ordinary People Build Extraordinary Brands, 2008
William E. Smith Institute for Association Research, Where the Winners Meet, 2006
Woolfe, Lorin - The Bible on Leadership, 2002
Wordstream.com

In addition, quotes from live presentations, books, blog posts, and articles not only made an impact on me when I first heard them but influenced the way I work. With thanks to the following authors, organizations, and historians who offered their perspective and consequently shaped my philosophies and approaches, I acknowledge them here:

Art of Charm
Berns, Gregory
Forbes, Glenn
Friedenberg, Edgar Z.
HSBC Bank
Nielson, Daniel
Nin, Anaïs
Naylor and Associates
Trenfor, Alexandra K.

Call or email nSight Marketing to discuss the value proposition process or other strategic communications issues.

Refer to www.breakthroughvalue.org to access Beyond the Book options, or simply use your mobile phone's camera to capture this QR code for easy reference.

nSight Marketing helps associations plan and execute relevant communications using proven frameworks.

melynn@nsightmarketing.com

www.breakthroughvalue.org

www.nsightmarketing.com

Made in the USA
Columbia, SC
31 October 2021